How Healthy is the C of E?

The Church Times Health Check

How Healthy is the C of E?

The Church Times Health Check

Edited by Malcolm Doney

Consultant Editor: Linda Woodhead

Illustrated by Dave Walker

CANTERBURY
PRESS
Norwich

© Hymns Ancient & Modern Ltd 2014

First published in 2014 by the Canterbury Press Norwich
Editorial office
3rd Floor, Invicta House,
108–114 Golden Lane,
London EC1Y 0TG.

Canterbury Press is an imprint of Hymns Ancient & Modern Ltd
(a registered charity)
13A Hellesdon Park Road, Norwich,
Norfolk, NR6 5DR, UK

www.canterburypress.co.uk

British Library Cataloguing in Publication data

A catalogue record for this book is available
from the British Library

978 1 84825 701 6

Printed and bound in Great Britain by
Ashford Colour Press,
Gosport, Hants

Contents

The case for treatment 115

About the Contributors

Vicky Beeching is a theologian, a writer, and a broadcaster, who is researching the ethics of technology.

Canon John Binns is the Vicar of St Mary the Great, Cambridge.

Peter Brierley is the founder of the Brierley Consultancy.

Andrew Brown writes on religion for The Guardian, and is the press columnist for the Church Times. He blogs at www.theguardian.com/commentisfree/andrewbrown

The Revd Dr Malcolm Brown is the Director of Mission and Public Affairs for the Archbishops' Council of the Church of England.

Charles Clarke is a former Home Secretary and is currently a visiting professor at the School of Political, Social and International Studies at the University of East Anglia.

The Rt Revd Graham Cray is the Archbishops' Missioner and leader of the Fresh Expressions team.

Madeleine Davies is Deputy News Editor of the Church Times.

The Revd Dr Maggi Dawn is Associate Professor of Theology and Literature, and Dean of Marquand Chapel, at the University of Yale.

Dr Abby Day is a senior research fellow, and lecturer in Anthropology of Religion at the University of Kent, Canterbury, and Reader in Race, Faith and Culture at Goldsmiths, London.

Adam Dinham is Professor of Faith and Public Policy and Director of the Faiths and Civil Society Unit, Goldsmiths, University of London.

The Revd Malcolm Doney is the Features Editor of the Church Times.

The Revd Dr Leslie J. Francis is the Professor of Religions and

Education at the University of Warwick, and Canon Treasurer and Canon Theologian at Bangor Cathedral.

Dr Philip Giddings is a lecturer in politics at the University of Reading, and chairs the House of Laity in the General Synod.

The Revd Dr David Goodhew is the director of the Centre for Church Growth Research, Cranmer Hall, Durham.

Paul Handley is the Editor of the Church Times.

Dr Margaret Harris is the Emeritus Professor of Voluntary Sector Organisation at Aston University, and Visiting Professor at Birkbeck, University of London.

The Ven. Bob Jackson is the director of the Centre for Church Growth, St John's College, Nottingham.

Simon Jenkins is editor of shipoffools.com, and tweets as @simonjenks.

The Rt Revd James Jones was formerly the Bishop of Liverpool, and now advises the Home Secretary on Hillsborough, and Waitrose on corporate social responsibility.

Susie Leafe is the director of Reform.

The Revd Dr Alison Milbank is an associate professor at the University of Nottingham in the department of Theology and Religious Studies and Priest Vicar at Southwell Minster.

Loretta Minghella is the Chief Executive Officer of Christian Aid.

Prebendary Anna Norman-Walker is Canon Missioner of Exeter Cathedral.

The Revd Philip North is the Rector of St Pancras Old Church, London, and a member of the General Synod.

Elizabeth Oldfield is Director of the think tank Theos.

The Revd Peter Ould blogs at www.peter-ould.net, and is founder of the Twitter aggregator, the Twurch of England.

Canon Professor Martyn Percy is the Principal of Ripon College, Cuddesdon.

Dennis Richards was head teacher of St Aidan's C of E High School, in Harrogate, for 23 years. He is now the chair of governors at St Oswald's C of E Primary Academy, in Bradford, and a governor of the David Young Community Academy in Leeds.

Dr Anna Rowlands is a lecturer in theology and ministry at King's College, London.

Dr Desmond Ryan is an Honorary Fellow in the School of Health in Social Science, University of Edinburgh.

Dr Anna Strhan is the Leverhume Early Career Fellow in the Department of Religious Studies at the University of Kent.

Stephen Timms is the MP for East Ham, and Shadow Minister for Employment.

The Revd Dr Graham Tomlin is Dean of St Mellitus College.

John Tuckett is programme manager for the emerging West Yorkshire & the Dales diocese. Previously, he led transformation programmes for the Ministry of Defence, and the Prison and Probation Services. Before that, he was a CEO of health authorities.

Dr David Voas is the Director of Research and Professor of Population Studies at the University of Essex. He is one of the authors of From anecdote to evidence: Findings from the Church Growth Research Programme 2011-2013.

Dr Robert Warner is Dean of Humanities at the University of Chester, where he is the Head of Theology and Religious Studies, and Professor of Religion, Culture, and Society.

Dr Linda Woodhead is the Professor of Sociology of Religion at Lancaster University.

Facing up to near-decimation

by Paul Handley

IT IS not all about the numbers, of course. In this book on the health of the Church of England, we begin by looking at trends in attendance. Official C of E figures suggest an overall decline of nine per cent in the past decade. We are not in the business of public relations: this is a sign of a body in poor health. If the C of E is to be regarded as a working body, it is able to do nine per cent less work than ten years ago. Less evangelism, less mission, less social work, less community action. Even giving, which for years bucked the trend, has been falling away in real terms for the past few years.

There are several reasons, beyond wistful optimism, why the C of E has failed to acknowledge this situation. First, it is not universal. One of the more interesting figures is that, in the decade to 2012, while 23 per cent of churches declined, 20 per cent grew. A narrow majority, 57 per cent, remained stable. Thus 77 per cent of churches have not experienced a crisis. Second, there is a justifiable scepticism about numerical measures of success. Faithfulness to Christ works to a different scale altogether. And, however universal Christ's offer, he gave no suggestion in his teaching that it would be taken up by all. Readers will be able to point to lively congregations with a weak grasp of theological understanding, and poorly attended churches where deep spirituality can be encountered. Third, social habits and attitudes have altered very quickly: regular weekly observance is no longer seen as necessary.

But numbers do matter. Churches are where, in general, faith starts, and is encouraged, and matures. The Word is preached, the sacraments are administered, and Christ is encountered. Smaller congregations mean fewer interactions between the people of God, and fewer opportunities to kindle the spark of Christian faith which exists in many on the edge of the Church — and, similarly, to be enriched by them. If trends continue, the burden of the building will become too much for the remnant, and the Church's most visible witness in that community will cease.

It is not all about age, of course. The Candlemas readings, above all others, celebrate the ancient faithfulness of Simeon and Anna. It is natural that men and women, as they age, pay more attention to spiritual and universal matters. The best churches are indifferent to age. But Christ's appeal is to people of every age, and his Church ought to reflect that. Like attracts like. A congregation that consists mainly of those aged over 65 will struggle to attract young people or families with children. If it loses that struggle, there will be no younger generation to take its place when the time comes.

Remedies exist, and their relative merits will be discussed on these pages. But a Church that denies that it is in crisis will not apply those remedies with the commitment that they will need in order to work.

THE contents of this book were commissioned by Malcolm Doney with the advice of Linda Woodhead and the assistance of Madeleine Davies. We are extremely grateful to the many contributors who produced work of exceptional quality at short notice. The pieces appeared in the *Church Times* between 31 January and 28 February 2014. They generated a good deal of interest and correspondence, a sample of which appeared in the paper in subsequent weeks (available on our archive).

The *Church Times* is committed to continuing the debate in the coming months, and reports regularly on initatives to grow the Church both numerically and spiritually. To follow the debate, I'm afraid there is no alternative but to subscribe to the paper (details on www.churchtimes.co.uk, or contact subs@churchtimes.co.uk). If a further incentive is needed, the *Church Times* carries a weekly Dave Walker cartoon.

how
healthy is
the C of E?

Time to get serious

Linda Woodhead has undertaken a series of surveys into religion and public life. She argues that her research shows a Church that must face up to the reality, or die

LORD CAREY, the former Archbishop of Canterbury, made headlines last November by telling the world that the Church of England was on the brink of extinction. There are reasons to take him seriously, and reasons to be seriously sceptical.

The props to Lord Carey's prognostication are sagging charts and drooping graphs, which extrapolate to a point when the Church disappears in a puff of smoke.

Yet trends do not always continue. Other factors usually come into play which render the future different from the past. Indeed, decline

SUNDAY MORNING

WE ARE DWINDLING

FED UP WITH CHURCH POLITICS

THE KIDS ARE PLAYING FOOTBALL

FOUND LAST WEEK'S SERMON UNCOMFORTABLE

OVERSLEPT

LATE NIGHT LAST NIGHT

NO ONE HERE TALKS TO ME

THE CHILDREN WON'T KEEP QUIET, AND PEOPLE STARE

SITTING IN THE COFFEE SHOP, READING THE PAPER

THE THURSDAY NIGHT HOME GROUP IS MY CHURCH

IN TROUBLE IF I DON'T BUILD THAT WARDROBE

itself is one such a factor: once it reaches a certain point, it triggers new choices and actions which alter the course of things.

Extrapolations to a religious zero point often rely on a dubious account of secularisation which sees religious decline as an inevitable outcome of modernisation. As more societies modernise, it becomes clearer that this outcome is far from inevitable. Think of religion in the "BRIC" [Brazil, Russia, India, China] countries, for example, or Korea and the Philippines in recent decades.

Nevertheless, Lord Carey is right to express concern. He presses us to look steadily, and honestly, at what research reveals about the Church of England in the UK today.

Here is an overview, drawing on large surveys I carried out with YouGov for the Westminster Faith Debates last year, analysed with Bernard Silverman, and supplemented by other data.

STILL SIGNIFICANT

WHAT is immediately clear is that Anglicanism is still a significant part of British society. About one third of the population identify as "C of E" or "Anglican", when asked what their religion is. If we average over all age-groups, the C of E remains the single largest religion or denomination in the country.

It still has advantages of which other religions can only dream: the history and heritage of a national Church; huge wealth and resources; a stake in about one third of schools; and deep insertion into the élite institutions of England — the monarchy, Parliament, the judiciary, public schools, Oxbridge, the armed forces, and so on.

DYING OUT

BUT it is equally clear that Anglicans are dying out. The third of the population who say that they are Anglican is heavily concentrated in older age-groups. Almost half of those over 60 are Anglicans, but by the time you get to people in their twenties, it is more like one in ten. Again, this is not inevitable. Not all religions are declining in Britain. The number of people identifying as Roman Catholic, for example, is fairly steady (probably boosted by migration), and most minority religions are doing a good job of transmission to younger generations.

As for actual church attendance, of those who say they are C of E, about 83 per cent say that they do not go to church other than very occasionally — perhaps for a funeral. The remaining 17 per cent are the churchgoers. Of these, about half attend weekly (those who go unless something stops them), and half attend less regularly (those who go if nothing stops them).

The accumulated evidence shows that attendance has now been declining for more than a century; became much steeper after the 1970s; and has not yet slowed down significantly.

TRANSMISSION FAILURE

WHAT we also see is that Anglican identity is not being transmitted from one generation to the next, and that this has been true for many decades. It is as true for older age groups as younger ones. But the decline — starkly demonstrated by the rise in people who said that they had "no religion" between the 2001 and 2011 Censuses — is so rapid that it cannot be accounted for simply by young people's not becoming Anglican like their parents. There must also be older people who disidentify with the C of E at some stage in life.

Belief in God is also declining, but not as fast as belonging. It is interesting to compare the graph below, which shows Anglicans by age, with the one opposite, which shows belief by age. What is clear is that numbers of people cease to belong, or identify with, the Church, but do not cease to believe. Atheism has been growing, but only a little — about one in five people are atheists. The rest of us believe in God with various degrees of certainty, or are not sure.

A TOXIC BRAND

THE important point is that younger people are still open to faith, but increasingly closed to the Churches, and indeed to "religion" in general. Religion has become a toxic brand. The most common

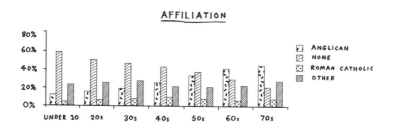

response among the young to the census question "What is your religion?" is now "None". Nearly half of young adults under 30 years of age say this. But less than half of "Nones" (43 per cent) say that they are atheists. What they reject more decisively than God is "religion".

Attitudes towards the Church of England are not encouraging. When asked if they view the Church as a positive force in society, only 18 per cent say "Yes", and only 14 per cent say "No". The majority (58 per cent) say "Neither", and the rest "Don't know". In other words, most people are ignorant of, or indifferent to, the Church rather than hostile.

As for the reasons for disapproval, older people are most likely to say that the Church is "boring and stuffy", but younger people now state a strong moral objection: "The Church is prejudiced — it discriminates against women and gay people."

VALUES GAP

THIS disconnect between wider social values and the Church's official teachings is striking. There has been a values revolution since the 1980s in Britain over the status and treatment of women, gay people, and children. The change has been swift, each generation being more likely than the one before to insist on equal treatment for the first two groups, and greater protection for children.

Among Christians under 45 years of age, for example, less than 30 per cent think that same-sex marriage is wrong, and an absolute majority think it is positively right (the rest "Don't know").

This results in a gulf in values between over-60s and under-50s. The Church is officially on the side of the former, and set against a moral

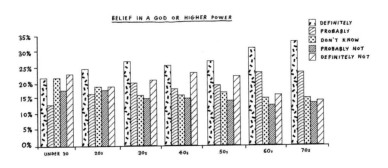

shift as significant as that which took place earlier in the 20th century in relation to race.

There is also a gap in values between Church and people on socio-political issues. Most people in Britain are now centre-right, and Anglicans are even further to the right than the majority. For example, nearly 70 per cent of "Anglicans" believe that the welfare system has created a culture of dependency — almost ten percentage points higher than the general population. But official church teaching is positioned much further to the left of both the population and, even more so, Anglicans.

This leaves the Church out of step with most of its supporters, as well as its detractors. It is both more left-wing in politics and more conservative in morals, and both more paternalist and more puritanical.

This values gap is certainly a reason for decline, but so is distance and indifference, given that each generation is increasingly unchurched. Only half the population say that they have had any contact with the Church in the past year, and the most common reason (given by 20 per cent) is for a funeral. Thus many people only know of the Church indirectly — through entertainment and news media, for example.

'The Church's greatest failure has been its refusal to take decline seriously'

AREAS OF GROWTH

DESPITE overall decline, there are some parts of the Church that are regarded positively. Reasons given are that it is "integral to English culture", "an ethical voice in society", and "part of our heritage".

Areas of wider Anglican success include chaplaincy (school chaplains are being actively recruited by many new academies, for example); some voluntary bodies with Anglican input; Christian Aid, the Children's Society and other charities; cathedrals; and schools.

In the congregational realm, there are also some areas of growth, as Peter Brierley (*page 20*) and Madeleine Davies (*page 32*) point out. There is clearly no single magic bullet. Formulaic solutions will not fit an organisation as broad as the C of E. What works for the majority of Anglicans who are irregular attenders is not what attracts enthusiasts.

The recent rapid decline in Anglican baptisms, weddings, and, increasingly, funerals, is therefore particularly serious, since this is the Church's core business, and of enormous importance to what has traditionally been a Church for the whole of society rather than just for the most committed churchgoers.

The Church's greatest failure in our lifetime has been its refusal to take decline seriously. The situation is now so grave that it is no longer enough simply to focus on making parts grow again. The whole structure needs to be reviewed from top to toe, and creative and courageous decisions need to be made.

Mixed outlook ahead

Attendance is certainly declining, says the veteran religion researcher *Peter Brierley*, but it is not all doom and gloom

IN ITS general forecast for the year ahead, *The World in 2014*, the editor of *The Economist* makes the sensible observation that "forecasts are as important as the decisions they inform."

Assessing what is currently happening, and what might happen as a consequence, is fraught with difficulty. But this was courageously tackled by the actuaries asked by the Church of England about future attendance. The First Church Estates Commissioner, Andreas Whittam Smith, in the July 2012 General Synod meeting in York, said that forecasts indicated that numbers would decrease to half a million by 2030, and by 90 per cent of the 2007 weekly attendance by 2057.

Both those figures represent **a severe decline** (*see figure 1, opposite*) for the years to 2030, broken down by age. It is clear that reaching those aged under 30 needs urgent attention. It is against that background that we evaluate the stories of encouragement where quality evangelism and church growth are taking place.

Two elements are 90 per cent likely: first, the overall numbers will continue to decline; second, the percentage of those who are 65 and over will increase. While some denominations are growing, even collectively they are not as big as the Church of England, which represented a quarter — 26 per cent — of the total attendance in 2012.

The only denomination of comparable size — and, in fact, slightly larger — is the Roman Catholic Church, but it, too, is declining, not growing (except slightly in London). It is also equally clear that, while most older people continue to attend church while they can, the numbers of young people joining the Church are simply too few to replace those who die.

One conversion to four deaths is the broad, overall equation from the past decade. Within that broad context, therefore, it has to be asked: where, and for whom, is the Church growing?

THE **Pentecostals are growing**, largely because of the enthusiasm of black churches in urban areas. The Redeemed Christian Church of God, for example, started its first church in 1993. It is now the third largest Pentecostal denomination in the UK; it had 100,000 members in 2012, across 500 churches.

The Pentecostals accounted for 12 per cent of total church attendance in England in 2012 — double their percentage in 1990. They are especially growing among black church families, so among adults and children up to, perhaps, 50 years of age.

Immigrant churches are also growing, especially in London, where there are more than 200 of them. This phenomenon has not (yet) spread widely to other cities. The Roman Catholics have been especially strong in starting churches for the many language groups coming from Roman Catholic countries (which is why they are growing in London). These attract mostly adult immigrants, 60 per cent of whom are 20 to 44.3 years of age.

Some of the **larger churches are growing,** particularly in London, where young people in their twenties are fairly numerous, and twice as likely to attend church as in other parts of England. Why are these churches, many of which are Anglican, popular? Part of the answer may lie in their application of biblical content, contemporary and

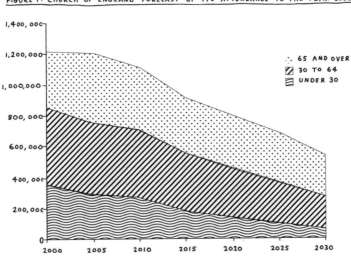

FIGURE 1: CHURCH OF ENGLAND FORECAST OF ITS ATTENDANCE TO THE YEAR 2030

21

flexible models of worship, and a lively, outgoing congregation.
Fresh Expressions, under various names, are growing. The expected **growth of Messy Church** (*see figure 2*) is remarkable. Half of those who attend them are probably already included in figures elsewhere, but the other half are new, non-church, or returned-to-church people.

Half of the forecast figure for 2020 would account for five per cent of church attendance then. Sixty per cent of their attendance is adult; 40 per cent is children.

BETH KEITH, a Church Army researcher, alongside George Lings, has been looking at places that appeal especially to those under the age of 30. Most of these are partly, or wholly, outside established denominations. She describes them as follows.

There are **"informal" churches**, meeting "more often around the dining table than in the church building". These are small communities, reaching young adults who often have no prior faith or church experience.

"Church-planting hubs" are "contemporary services for young adults, organised alongside community based activities, with an emphasis on personal missional activities. These reach educated, middle-class young adults with a Christian upbringing, often located in student areas."

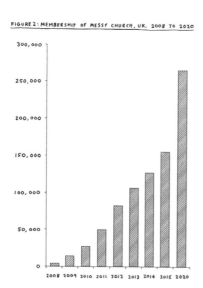

FIGURE 2: MEMBERSHIP OF MESSY CHURCH, UK, 2008 TO 2020

"Youth church grown up" are organisations "which began life as youth ministries. Ten years on, their members are growing up, but not connecting to other forms of church. They are considering how their church could become a place for young adults."

"Deconstructed churches" meet regularly, but not necessarily, on Sunday, and probably not in a church building.

"They place a high value on community, with church practices based around meals. Prayer, thanksgiving, communion, and discipleship happen during the meal."

"Churches on the margins" reach "young adults marginalised by wider society, from non-church backgrounds. Many in these churches struggle with illness, mental health, addictions, suicide, homelessness, **'The future may not be as bleak as it is forecast'** violence, and criminal activity. These churches focus on transforming lives, meeting together over food, and providing practical support."

"Context-shaped churches" have regular gatherings, not necessarily weekly or on a Sunday. "While traditional elements of church, such as communion, teaching, worship, prayer, discipleship, and fellowship are evident, there is often no clear service, preaching, or singing. By using a range of spaces, these churches cross the sacred/secular divide."

THERE is also growth in other denominations, among the independent and new church sectors; but, because there are also closures, they balance out. The **Orthodox churches are growing** steadily, but represent a small proportion of total church attendance (one per cent in 2012). The Orthodox are especially strong with those aged 30 to 44.

And there is a further facet of interest in **urban areas**, where, while we cannot exactly observe growth, there is a much slower rate of

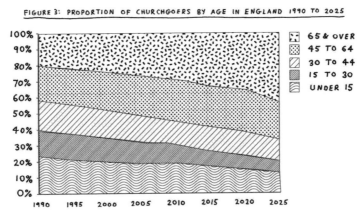

FIGURE 3: PROPORTION OF CHURCHGOERS BY AGE IN ENGLAND 1990 TO 2025

decline than elsewhere. Taking towns at random, Luton had a church attendance of eight per cent in 2012, against six per cent in the rest of Bedfordshire; in Cambridge, the rate is seven per cent to five per cent in Cambridgeshire; in Macclesfield, nine per cent to six per cent in Cheshire; Carlisle, eight per cent against six per cent, and so on.

Such **urban growth is not uniform or universal**, but there is enough of a pattern to suggest that some churches outside London can have a significant impact, attracting more of those under the age of 45.

Weighing up these movements statistically is not easy. Figure 3 puts the percentage of churchgoers under the age of 30 at 20 per cent by 2025, and those who are 65 or over at 43 per cent. These percentages compare with 15 and 46 per cent respectively for 2025 in figure 1, showing that, when other denominations are taken into consideration, the future may not be as bleak for the Church of England as the actuaries forecast.

Why young people turn their backs on church

It is not the style of worship, the age of the congregation, or the lack of faith that turns young people away, argues *Robert Warner*

THERE are a number of standard reasons given for the drop-out rate of young people from church. They include: inconvenient times of Sunday services; predictable preaching; an average congregational age of 50-plus; and alienation from church culture, from liturgical verbosity to superficial jollity.

Secularisation theorists have long argued that the cumulative impact of the social processes that marginalise religion is that people simply lose interest. It is not that most have become fervent atheists: they just cannot be bothered to "do God".

Christianity and the University Experience was a three-year study into undergraduates who describe themselves as Christian. We could have imposed a definition of "Christian" that was credal, or emphasised being a regular communicant. Instead, we asked those who chose to describe themselves as Christian to tell us their moral convictions and religious practices.

It turned out that nine out of ten Christian students are not in Christian Unions, and the vast majority rarely or never attend church during term time.

The 1960s moral revolution has had a double impact. First, the traditional moral constraints of the Church were overturned. Then the Church increasingly came under judgement from the new moral consensus. People no longer consider themselves to be behaving "immorally", let alone "living in sin". Instead, they have embraced a new morality, and it is the Church that is now considered immoral.

Our results among students, and Linda Woodhead's parallel studies among adults, suggest that the moral consensus has shifted irrevocably — not just among non-Christians, but among Christians, too. These Christians take it for granted that sex is no longer confined to marriage; contraception and abortion are standard interventions; living together is sensible; and those who are gay should have fully equal rights and the opportunity to marry.

They think it is common sense that there should be women and gay bishops. They also consider voluntary euthanasia infinitely more humane than doctrinaire enforcement of prolonged suffering on the terminally ill.

ONLY Anglicans and neo-Pentecostals recruit significant numbers of new churchgoers among students. For Anglicans, those recruited are far outnumbered by the drop-outs; but these new Anglicans mostly attend Evangelical and Charismatic churches, and uphold traditional Christian morality. Even here there are signs of change: 60 per cent of today's Evangelical students consider that gay sex is always wrong. That is a solid majority, but not many years ago it would surely have been almost 100 per cent.

The impact of university on Anglicanism is therefore twofold. For the majority of "hidden Christians", Sunday attendance becomes infrequent, and they reject traditional morality, but their Christian identity and spirituality remain important.

For the conservative minority, Sunday attendance is very frequent, their Church should militantly defend traditional morality without any compromise, and many doubt that the "hidden Christians" are really Christian at all.

The Reformation was a paradigm shift, as was the abolition of slavery, and now we have entered another mega-shift of Christian consciousness. Young Christians have embraced a paradigm shift in morality. A new set of moral convictions has become self-evident and compelling.

This is far more important than the crisis of contemporaneity which makes church services seem boring and old-fashioned. From the perspective of the new paradigm, the Church has become a bastion of reactionary attitudes, and moral blindness. The Church has lost its moral authority among Christians, let alone in society, because it has lost its moral credibility, and is seen to defend indefensible prejudice.

FOR some clergy and bishops, this new moral consensus is painfully difficult to accept as authentically Christian. The priesthood, however, no longer has moral authority over the laity. Long before David Cameron made gay marriage illegal in Anglican churches, the hidden Christians had made up their minds to the contrary.

This remarkably rapid evolution of Christian morality, mirroring the broader moral revolution in Western society, belies the meta-narrative of dogmatic secularisation theory. Christianity turns out to be more durable than many expected, and more capable of cultural adaptation.

While the hidden Christians have overturned traditional Christian moral teaching, they continue to practise personal spirituality. At university, nearly half of all Christians pray more than weekly. In some universities, this means one in four of all their students are praying regularly. That is an awful lot of praying by a supposedly secular generation.

From the old paradigm, senior clergy want the Church to be more engaging, without softening its traditional moral absolutism. One recently described modern Britain as "floundering amid meaningless anxiety and despair". I find little evidence of this existential angst the other side of the paradigm shift.

New paradigm Christians, unless they are Roman Catholic by birth, will almost always identify to some extent with their national Church. Many pray regularly in private, and affirm confidently their new Christian morality. But they won't often be found in the pews.

In Richard Hooker's terms, these hidden Christians are surely part of the Established Church. But will the Church seek to include them, and give them a voice? Or will the Church alienate them still further, entrenching the absolutist morality of the old Christian paradigm?

A language designed for insiders

John Binns has an ambivalent relationship with
Common Worship, and believes it is ultimately a barrier to
would-be churchgoers

THE website whychurch.org reviewed statistics of church membership over the past ten years, and concluded that there are four categories of people that the Church is failing to reach: men, the young, the poor, and Christians. The surprising last category arises from the growing number of people who, when asked, say that they are Christian, but do not go to church. They are the believers who do not belong.

This requires all of us who plan and conduct church worship to ask whether we have failed to identify, and offer, a liturgy that engages and articulates the faith of our generation. And, since this has been the period when we have become accustomed to the liturgical style and context of *Common Worship 2000*, this soul-searching must include our experience of this book, which has shaped the worshipping life of our Church.

Most of us have a list of the parts that we love, and which move us, and also the phrases and prayers that irritate. We find that some services work, while others need revision. The marriage service meets with general approval, but, as the recent public debate has revealed, we find some statements in the baptism service difficult.

Although it is interesting for those of us who worship to swap stories and experiences, and for the Liturgical Commission to devise new forms of service, this misses the point of why the liturgy of the Church of England, and especially *Common Worship*, fails to address this generation. It is an activity for those already inside the doors.

Let us start by asking how we actually use *Common Worship*. At my church, we consider that our main act of worship is parish communion, on Sunday morning, and the baptism service that takes place within it. For this, we use *Common Worship*, with its wide range of options, to enable us to derive a form of service that fits our own circumstances.

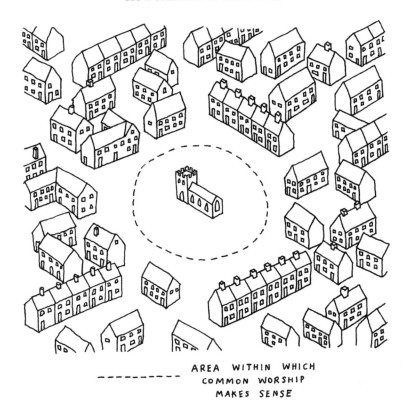

AREA WITHIN WHICH
COMMON WORSHIP
MAKES SENSE

We also offer choral evensong, and usually matins as well. This attracts visitors, and others who attend more occasionally, who would not see themselves as full members. We use the Book of Common Prayer, employed within the range of the Anglican choral tradition.

THEN there are special services: the school end-of-term services, the launch of a new charitable organisation, the shoppers' carol service. We devise our own order of service for each occasion.

So, for us, *Common Worship* and parish communion go together, and I suspect that that is the case for others, too. *Common Worship* affirms and strengthens the eucharistic life of the Church; so it makes the assumption that a church is a defined and identified group of

29

people who form a community, and gives a language to express this identity, and a ritual character to give it shape.

But the problem with any community is that, while there are some within it who value the comfort and reassurance it provides, there are also others who are outside. Any liturgy, or form of words drafted for use by one community, will exclude all those who are not included. If we see the church primarily as a community, then we are setting up a system that excludes just as much as it includes.

If *Common Worship* serves a defined Christian community, does it serve those who are outside? Is it building a faithful gospel witness, or is it using the theological language of eucharist and communion to justify and facilitate the withdrawal from an aggressively secular society into the safe haven of a clearly defined community?

I have just returned from a fascinating visit to the only sub-Saharan African country with a long history of Christian faith: Ethiopia. It took me a while to grasp that their churches are completely different from ours; in fact, they are not churches in our sense at all.

Instead of buildings in which Christians gather for worship, they are holy enclosures with several different parts: a holy of holies, to which only clergy have access; a place where choir and worship leaders perform the sacred songs; a hall where young people are taught the faith; and a large space outside where people read and pray.

At festivals, there will be different kinds of worship continuing all night — sometimes with two or more going on simultaneously. People go to whatever bits they want, and very few go to all.

POST-MODERN England is a different kind of society from rural Ethiopia, but there may be something that we can learn from them. Worship is not a catch-all activity that must be conducted in a style laid down by the church authorities. It is diverse, varied, simultaneous, and unexpected. A post-modern church needs to discover a post-liturgical style of worship.

We need to recognise that places matter. Far more people in the UK relate to the church building itself than come to the worship within it. We need to think more about the part we play as a custodian of national sacred space.

Occasions matter. People come to church when they have something to say or do: this may be the birth of a child, or the death of a loved one, the end of a school term, or the launch of a new organisation. Marking special occasions is how most people worship.

I value my participation in *Common Worship* parish communion on a Sunday morning. It is fine as a starting point; but we need to discover forms of worship that can speak to that majority of Anglicans who find that our liturgy does not speak to them.

Ten things

from the C of E's church-growth research programme.

Report by *Madeleine Davies*

EIGHTEEN months ago, three research teams were commissioned by the Archbishops to explore growth in the Church of England. The report, *From Anecdote to Evidence*, was launched on 16 January. Here are the headlines:

1. The Church is losing young people

Just 2.2 per cent of people aged 16-19 attend monthly or more often. This falls to 1.4 per cent among those aged 20-24. Affiliation statistics are slightly higher (8.2 per cent and 7.6 per cent respectively).

2. Parents do not prioritise passing on their faith

When presented with a list of "qualities that children can be encouraged to learn at home", and asked to select what they considered to be "especially important", just 11 per cent of Anglicans selected religious faith.

3. Decline is not uniform, and there is no single recipe for growth

In the decade up to 2010, 27 per cent of churches declined, 55 per cent remained stable, and 18 per cent grew. While there is no "single recipe" for growth, there are a number of "ingredients" that are associated with growth and can be applied in any setting.

4. Cathedrals are growing

Weekly attendance at cathedrals grew by 35 per cent between 2002 and 2012, while weekday attendance more than doubled.

5. Leadership is critical

A survey of clergy found a strong correlation between those clergy who prioritise numerical growth and those clergy whose churches grew in numbers.

6. Good-quality lay leadership is linked to growth

A church where volunteers are involved in leadership, and where tasks are rotated regularly, is much more likely to be growing, especially where younger members and new members are included.

7. Fresh Expressions are working

A study of ten dioceses found that about 21,000 people attended a Fresh Expression — the numerical equivalent of a new, medium-sized diocese. Research suggests that 40 per cent of those attending are non-churched.

8. Growing churches are often found in cities

While attendance as a proportion of the population is often highest in rural areas, growth is hard to achieve here. Growth is often found in cities, where relatively few people are Anglican.

9. Success is not a function of churchmanship or worship style

Self-reported growth is associated with Evangelical, conservative, and Charismatic tendencies. Yet Professor David Voas, who led one of the research teams, found that "controlling for other characteristics nearly always reduces churchmanship to insignificance".

10. Amalgamations are strongly associated with decline

A single church with one leader is more likely to grow than churches grouped together. The more churches amalgamate together, the more the risk of decline increases.

www.churchgrowthresearch.org.uk

What do we believe?

Precisely what Christians mean by 'belief' differs according to their tradition, *Anna Strhan* discovers

WHEN the the computer scientist Sir Tim Berners-Lee was guest-editing the *Today* programme on BBC Radio 4, on 26 December 2013, he asked that an atheist should provide *Thought for the Day*.

Andrew Pakula, the atheist minister of a north-London Unitarian church, said in his "Thought": "While I don't literally believe the stories underlying Christmas, I do very much believe in its most important messages." He later criticised the BBC's approach to religion, tweeting: "I'd say I have faith although I'm an atheist. BBC says this is impossible — except for Buddhists."

What it means to be religious, and a Christian, is often framed through the lens of "belief". Debates about Christianity's social significance refer not only to statistics on church attendance, but to surveys demonstrating percentages of the population believing in God, heaven, hell, etc.

Yet Dr Pakula's questioning of how "faith" relates to belief in a supernatural deity raises questions about precisely what we mean when we use the term "belief", and about the part that belief plays in the lives of those who attend church.

I AM a sociologist who conducts fieldwork in different kinds of churches. I am often struck by the way the significance accorded to "belief", and the different styles that belief takes, varies across traditions.

When carrying out research within Evangelical Anglican churches, I found that Charismatic Christians expressed the meaning of belief somewhat differently from conservative Evangelicals.

For conservative Evangelicals, to be a Christian is — first and foremost — to be a believer. Belief, in this case, is understood primarily in terms of propositional knowledge: in other words, "belief that" certain statements of knowledge are true.

One student said: "Feeling God as present — I don't know what that feels like. I have knowledge, and . . . I believe that God is always there watching over us, and that his love extends to all of us."

They also saw belief as relational — what we might describe as "belief in" — centring on a relationship with God which requires obedient submission. This is bound up with beliefs about the correct ordering of human relationships. For example, one minister preached that "God rules: he's delegated his authority to the head of the family; and then the father and the mother — under the headship of the man — are in authority over the children."

YET, contrary to popular stereotypes of Evangelicals as always certain of their beliefs, and perhaps contrary to how they might respond to a survey, I found that, as I spent time with them, they articulated awareness of doubts. And, in sermons, ministers described doubt as a recurring feature of the Christian life.

Individuals I spoke to described doubt as an uneasy state. For example, one woman said that it was "this huge black hole of, 'Is it really true?'" Church leaders encouraged particular practices to encourage individuals to "cling" to their beliefs.

One minister said: "The default position for all of us as Christians is drift. We don't have to do anything to drift; if we don't do anything, we do drift, but we've got to make an effort to keep going, to continue.

"The old line people used to say to me: 'Read your Bible and pray every day' — when you chat to somebody about why they've drifted into all sorts of mess, almost invariably you can trace it back to "Well, I was in a busy patch, and my Bible-reading and prayer went out the window.'"

Individuals I came to know also knotted each other into relationships of accountability — for example, texting friends if they did not see them at church — through which they established expectations of regular church and Bible-study-group attendance. Through these communal and individual practices, they worked to form themselves and each other as believers.

THE Charismatic Anglicans I have spent time with emphasise "spontaneity" and "messiness" as central to their relational believing. A sense of intimate relationship with God, and conviction in God's un-bounded, cherishing love, is at the core. Singing songs for long periods, and the intense emotional experiences associated with these, are key practices. The language expressing this intimacy with God is primarily that of love and friendship.

The term "belief" is also used to reinforce a sense of a pluralist public sphere, when addressing those outside the Church. They use phrases such as "as Christians, we believe" to articulate a consciousness of their addressing others with different convictions.

In speaking about their practical social engagements, Charismatics' belief is also infused with the language of hope. One church leader, for example, quoted the writer Anne Lamott to describe her work with local parents: "Hope begins in the dark; the stubborn hope that if you just show up, and try to do the right thing, the dawn will come."

NON-EVANGELICAL and "mainstream" Anglicans may be less likely to describe themselves as "believers". An exchange between a Roman Catholic philosopher and a liberal Anglo-Catholic university chaplain evokes this. The philosopher told the chaplain: "The problem with you Anglicans is that you're so vague about your beliefs." The Anglican replied: "And why is that a problem?"

'Individuals knotted themselves into relationships of accountability'

There is a wider latitude of belief among non-Evangelical and liberal Anglicans. Professor Linda Woodhead's YouGov survey demonstrates that most churchgoing Anglicans do express a "belief in God", but they do not take their moral authority from religious leaders or scriptures, but prefer to make up their own minds.

Regardless of the extent to which Anglicans think of themselves as believers, different practices of believing are deeply interwoven into the mundane rhythms of what they do when they meet together in church.

Any act of believing means an orientation towards an "other" — whether God, or people — who transcends the self; and towards a past and a future beyond, but folded within, the present moment.

Perhaps it is in this gesture of the self turning outwards that belief, in its very diverse forms, remains significant in Anglican lives today.

Why a parish?

Desmond Ryan asks whether parishes are in a position
to adapt effectively in order to address the spiritual energy
of their parishioners

"WHAT is a parish for?" It is an easy question to ask, but an impossible one to answer. "Parish" has always been a derivative idea, emanating from, and established by, the Church, especially after it came to dominate medieval Europe through its near-monopoly of thought and writing, in rivalrous partnership with Christian monarchs.

Western or Eastern, Roman Catholic or Protestant, the Church is the whole; the parish is the part. Hence, constitutionally, the parish has been organised, and still functions, to serve the Church.

In spiritual terms, its life derives from its membership (in the fullest sense) of the Church as the Body of Christ. As every parish was an organ of the Body of Christ, every individual was a parishioner — a notion still subscribed to by the established Churches of Northern Europe, and by the Roman Catholic Church for its faithful, who are entrusted by the bishop (charged, as successor to the Apostles, to "Feed my sheep") to the care of the parish priest.

What is most significant about the parish today are the functions it is *not* performing. The legacy of resources in a single location inherited from a thousand years of geography, architecture, cultural prescription, and social policy is insufficient to tame and exploit the powerful currents flowing through the homes and public spaces within the parish bounds.

Professor Linda Woodhead's Religion and Society project has revealed just how much intensely spiritual energy is to be found in every corner of the country. It is common knowledge that little of this is powering new waves of vitality in parochial churches.

HOW can this be? How can spiritual energy not seek expression in religious institutions? By way of (a necessarily brief) answer, let me propose a working distinction between two forms of spiritual energy, utilising two quintessentially Christian concepts: the Body of Christ, and the Kingdom of God.

Commandeering them for sociological purposes, I distinguish them as follows. The Body of Christ is institutionalised, established by authority of the supreme author, Christ himself. It is historical and hierarchical, with recognised legal instruments and defined social roles. It lives through cult and prayer, and liturgy and sacraments, hence it almost always uses specially constructed buildings, authoritative books, musical instruments, and other materials. It organises the day, the week, and the year.

It is, in principle, inclusive, but is built on continuing membership of a social community, lifelong and stretching forward down the generations. This membership gives a socially accepted religious identity, and is made visible by attendance at corporate worship, and by receiving the sacraments.

The community is focused on, served by, and responsive to, a pastor, ordained to that position by the Church, who builds the community as a replication and continuing outflow of Christ the good shepherd's loving service to others.

The community reproduces itself "ecclesiogenically" through family membership, education, and local recruitment — nowadays distinctly low-key, judging from my research in the Roman Catholic Birmingham archdiocese in 1991 (*The Catholic Parish*, Sheed & Ward, 1996).

In short, the energies that build up parishes as the Body of Christ work locally through enduring networks of individuals with specific social identities, social positions, and local residence — for many it may well be their "second home".

BY THE "Kingdom of God", in contrast, I mean those spiritual energies that are diffuse rather than embodied; which "blow where they will" and touch people unexpectedly, and in unpredictable ways; which bring them to self-awareness, and self-questioning; which disrupt established patterns, and commitments, and set people off down new paths, often radically different from what went before.

These energies empower them to make contact with others for one or more stages of their journey, albeit that such contacts are relatively fleeting. It is a journey of permanent transition, fuelled by the search for meaning and truth — for each individual — and by the power of the word, in a plethora of scriptures and hymns, often transmitted through recordings and on the web.

The journey takes people through a succession of learning experiences — especially meditation, and other centring practices — but also such occasions for self-discovery as ashrams, retreats, Enneagrams, Myers-Briggs, Ignatian spirituality, the Diamond Approach, and myriads more.

Compared with the parish, often the beneficiary of centuries of donations from believers, this journey can be financially expensive. Most of these occasions for personal spiritual growth make their fruits available through the market, and, while few are frankly exploitative, preachers and teachers have a living to make.

Healers, too; one of the distinctive things about these energies is their lack of specificity, as likely to manifest in practices of the body as of the soul, in a desire to be whole as much as a desire to be "saved". It is not the least significant feature of complementary and alternative therapies that they attract to their studios, as both users and practitioners, refugees from both the religious and the health-care systems of late modernity.

To sum up: those pursuing the "Kingdom of God" as here presented do, indeed, seem to be living in a quantum and relativistic world of discontinuous "events" that exhibit process and change:

"For the modern view process, activity and change are the matter of fact. . . Thus, all the interrelations of matters of fact must involve transition in their essence. All realisation involves implication in the creative advance."(*Nature and Life*, A. N. Whitehead, CUP, 1934).

THIS contrast of cultural forms taken by spiritual energies is necessarily a caricature. But some such extreme statement is required to make clear what I believe to be the case: that we have been living through an explosion in "the creative advance" of social relationships, cultural expression, and spiritual values which has already made this era into the most rapid, intense, and fundamental "reformation" there has ever been.

And it has passed the parish by. The parishes of the hierarchical and Established Churches of the UK are failing to bring to parochial earth spiritual energies that saturate their social space. Theological purists may dismiss these energies as "wacky", or of doubtful origin; but, surely, so much rebirth and connection, such vitality and desire for fullness of humanity, cannot be evoked by forces that are completely spurious?

Theological indifference to these "anthropogenic" energies prompts the fear that the Church's lack of theory of its general social context makes it effectively blind in that environment.

To the parish as the local embodiment of the Christian Church we should apply Reg Revans's axiom: that "for any organism to survive, its rate of learning must be equal to, or greater than, the rate of change in the environment." Failing such learning, contextual change causes "extinction" of life-forms as, in effect, adapted to yesterday's environment. Is the parish such a life-form?

Church growth for atheists

While Christians seem to be abandoning the
Church, atheists are starting their own, with some
success. *Simon Jenkins* reports

THIS time last year, I went one cold Sunday to an empty shell of a
church in an area of Hackney, London, called De Beauvoir Town. The
church, a Victorian behemoth long deconsecrated, was a beautiful
wreck, with scaffolding outside and crumbling plaster inside.

It looked like church as you might imagine it after the Apocalypse:
the faithful gone, the organ falling to bits, the stone reredos missing
chunks of masonry, the glory departed. The old place had been
cannibalised by a school, the side aisles and upstairs balcony crudely
screened off with plasterboard.

Actually, forget the Apocalypse. This could just be the present reality
of the Church in lingering decline.

But, on this Sunday, the building had found a new congregation.
As I turned in at the church gate, a couple of bright young things
greeted me with smiles and leaflets and directed me towards the
building. There was a crowd at the door, and I experienced a surreal
moment of queuing to get into church. Had I slipped into a parallel
universe?

I could easily have been witnessing a church-plant, with a couple of
hundred keen Evangelicals from Holy Trinity, Brompton, bused in;
but, instead, this was the launch event of the Sunday Assembly (the
new "godless" congregation or "atheist church"). The service came
complete with a secular sermon, plus hymns — not by Mrs Cecil
Alexander, or even by Graham Kendrick, but by Freddie Mercury and
Stevie Wonder.

I found the dissonance between failed church building and vibrant
atheist gathering both striking and challenging. Crowds of atheists
happily chatting over post-service cups of tea, and enthusiastically
taking over where Christians had faded away did not exactly fit the
script that Jesus laid out at the great commission.

The Sunday Assembly is perhaps the most churchlike of several recent ventures where atheism has got itself up in the borrowed clothes of religion. This has mostly been done in an ironic way, but the Sunday Assembly is a departure, because — although it markets itself with a great deal of comedy — it has embraced the format of church sincerely, often to the point of scandalising fellow atheists.

ONE of them, the pop philosopher Alain de Botton, complains that the Sunday Assembly has merely copied what he set up across town at the School of Life. The School has run "Sunday sermons" for several years, and getting the audience to sing pop songs, just as congregations sing hymns, was probably invented there.

Other atheists have hosted events that sound like church — such as the comedian Robin Ince's annual Nine Lessons and Carols for Godless People, a stage show that brings together comics and scientists — but there is not much of a nod to religion beyond the eye-catching title.

The part played by comedians in the visible rise of New Atheism seems to be significant in all this. It looks as if a number of stand-up comedians have taken on the part of the preacher, or even the evangelist, as they pour hilarious invective on the real and perceived contradictions of faith. Ricky Gervais and Frankie Boyle have been especially effective in turning the scorn of Richard Dawkins into comedy.

I do not think that it would be a stretch to argue that a whole generation of young people are laughing their way into atheism, agnosticism, or plain indifference towards God.

The comedian Frank Skinner, in a public conversation with then Archbishop Rowan Williams in 2011, talked about how, in almost every stand-up routine he heard, the comedian would make time to ridicule God and religion. Skinner, a Roman Catholic, believed that this was alarming, because it widely discredited faith, and he teasingly asked the Archbishop — as if he still had the power of his medieval predecessors — "What are you going to do about it?"

ATHEIST church was born when comedy gig segued seamlessly into godless service. The founding parents of the Sunday Assembly, Sanderson Jones and Pippa Evans, both seasoned stand-ups, came up with the idea on a drive home after performing. But, although the Assembly's services are run with huge energy and lashings of comedy, the underlying aim of the project, to "'live better, help often, wonder more", is heartfelt and serious.

The services are a warm and barnstorming celebration of life rather than a chance to have a go at religion. "How atheist should our Assembly be?" Jones asks. "The short answer to that is: not very."

This positive approach, coupled with regular services where people can sing, listen to a talk, reflect on their lives, be entertained, and meet others — all without the outrageous claims of religious belief — appeals to a segment of the 48 per cent of young adults who wrote "No religion" on their UK census forms in 2011.

It offers all the good and human things about church, but without the requirement to sign up to a creed — and that is very appealing in our culture right now.

The Sunday Assembly, a New Year blog post on its website states, now has 28 active congregations around the world — including several in the UK — which attract numbers that would be the envy of many parish churches. The movement is only one year old, and it is hard to predict whether the founders' ambitious plans for growth will work out, but the movement does not look as if it's about to disappear.

The Assembly in New York City even had its own church split, when some members were being more determinedly atheist than others. That schism surely proves that atheist church is just like real church, and is here to stay.

NOW WE WILL STAND TO
NOT SAY THE CREED

What gets me out of bed on Sunday

Despite, or maybe because of, the Church's cultural irrelevance, *Vicky Beeching* continues to sit in the pews

MY ALARM clock cracked as it hit the wall at high speed. Its beeps morphed into strangled, robotic squeaks as it malfunctioned and died on the bedroom carpet. I had propelled it across the room when it awoke me, such was my lack of excitement about getting up early on a Sunday.

Sunday mornings are like the sleep equivalent of the last motorway service station for the next 50 miles. They convey the disturbing realisation that the next working week looms, and there is one final opportunity to hit the snooze button — or, in my case, turn the alarm clock into a projectile.

The Church has a tricky PR job — persuading the faithful to slough off the cocoon of a warm duvet, and make the trek to a Sunday service. Often, I prefer the idea of sleeping in, making gloriously tasty bacon sandwiches, and watching weekend TV. And yet I prise myself off my mattress and make the journey to the pews as regularly as I can.

WHY do I go? Sometimes, simply out of discipline and obedience — both of which are unfashionable concepts these days. There are, in fact, many aspects to churchgoing which seem unfashionable and culturally irrelevant. Some argue that these are reasons to condemn it as outdated, and destined to die off.

Conversely, I would suggest that some of the Church's greatest strengths lie in its lack of cultural relevance: after all, that has never been its primary calling. Sometimes, the required antidote to societal pitfalls lies not in mirroring the latest trends, but in radically counter-cultural practices.

Their apparent irrelevance makes them, bizarrely, highly relevant. They are a big part of what keeps me coming back, week after week, as I find them to be exactly what I need in this digital age.

So what are they? One is the renewal of our connection to locality. Online technology makes our lives increasingly virtual: shopping, talking, dating, work, and education increasingly happen in cyberspace. Being online brings vast benefits, but also diminishes our rootedness in a specific locale.

This digital gnosticism finds a helpful remedy in the concept of parish, as it roots worshippers in their specific, physical square mile of concrete or countryside.

SILENCE is another much-needed antidote that churchgoing offers. In a world that has never been noisier, silence brings perspective, and centres us. It is crucial for human well-being. Worship services often contain elements of silence which are difficult to find elsewhere. Other than a library, few other places give it hallowed space: even beauty spas or meditation centres frequently play musical soundtracks. People tend to find silence uncomfortable today, owing to its unfamiliarity, but worship services provide a rare and valuable chance to embrace its benefits.

Repetition is another of the hidden gems. Liturgy may seem boring: the same prayers and creeds are used week after week, year after year. Today, brevity and novelty are king. Yet repetitive liturgy offers something refreshing in a world that is comprised of 140-character sound-bites. It is an important reminder that good things often take time.

DOING life with extremely diverse people is another counter-cultural antidote that is offered by many churches. Social media can lead us to believe that we are surrounded by a kaleidoscopic, radically varied crowd. In reality, we often just follow a number of people similar to us.

Church, at its best, is a dramatically diverse melting-pot of humanity, united by a common faith. "But some of the people there are so annoying," one of my friends complained, as she described why she wanted to give up attending. Yet the fact that we have to learn to worship with people who are not like us is incredibly healthy. Online, we can retreat into our own silos, whereas local church forces us to spend regular time with those outside our comfort zone.

I am not saying that we should resist modernising church in healthy ways. I love carefully, prayerfully updated liturgical language. I would also like to see mobile technology introduced at points within services, to engage digital teens who find services increasingly alien. But cultural relevance must never become an end in itself. Nor, of course, should church become primarily about what we "get out of it": its ultimate purpose is not getting, but giving, as we offer up our worship. It is a two-way exchange, however, and can grow and develop us in surprising ways.

The reason why I climb out of my warm bed on a Sunday morning, and head to church, is because I believe that many of its seemingly irrelevant aspects are actually the potent antidotes needed to survive, and thrive, in this digital age. And that beats a lie-in and a bacon sandwich any day.

Help thou mine unbelief

Andrew Brown is no stranger to experiences of conversion, but it has never quite stuck. He explains why

MY TROUBLE with Christianity is that it is only true backwards. To take an example, here is a couplet from George Herbert: "Sin is that Press and Vice, which forceth pain To hunt his cruel food through every vein," and when I read it, two things happen almost at once.

The first is a stunned, visceral assent: a delight in the thought and its expression, and most of all in the way they are so perfectly united. The second is to note that it is not true. Pain is not always — or even often — the consequence of sin. My friend with the brain tumour and her husband are not being punished for anything anyone has done.

But suppose we read the couplet backwards — not as a description of the workings of sin in the world, but as a statement about the meaning of the word "sin", and about whatever it is that "forceth pain to hunt his cruel food through every vein".

Perhaps this is a distinction without a difference, but I think not. To read the couplet the first way is to treat "sin" as an almost scientific term: it becomes part of the chain of cause and effect, a name we give to an observable, predictable, and, in principle, even measurable pattern of events in the world. It becomes an explanatory hypothesis.

Used in this sense, we can postulate "sin" rather as we postulate the Higgs boson, and then go to see if it helps us to understand the world a bit better. But, in that sense, "sin" clearly does not exist. It is an epicycle, a meme, a failed would-be explanatory mechanism.

Read backwards, however, the couplet tells us something about the meaning of the word "sin". This is more interesting. There is a "Press and Vice, which forceth suffering through every vein" — we know this, because we see people and animals tortured all around us, usually by disease, but sometimes by deliberate wanton act.

This is clearly something that has evolved, in the sense that the earth was once lifeless, and for billions of years without conscious life or feeling. So there is something in the way the universe is which has produced the capacity to suffer, and maintained it and refined it through innumerable generations. Calling that something "sin" illuminates what the word might mean. It gives the doctrine of "Original Sin" something real to refer to, and makes it worth thinking about.

' I may be a sinner, but I don't want to be mistaken for a bishop'

THINKING about doctrine in this way is not a habit that I am ever going to kick. I have done it almost as far back as I can remember. Perhaps the most shameful thing I will admit to publicly is that I won a scholarship to Marlborough on the strength of my essay in the Divinity exam.

But I remember, too, the feeling when I had finished writing: that I had no idea at all whether any of it was true. It was just a rhetorical exercise, in a mode in which I happen to be naturally gifted. So I concluded that the man who marked it so highly must be bluffing, too.

Subsequent, banal experiences with Christians who were stupid, cruel, smug, pharisaical, and otherwise human cemented this disillusionment. I could read the Prayer Book, and love it, but, when I attempted the Bible, I would recoil, simply unable to believe that anyone would take it as the word of God. When people describe themselves as "Bible-believing Christians", I can attach no meaning to the words, except as a label: it is like being "flag-believing Britons". Similarly, I do not know what it could possibly mean to believe in a Creator.

None of this inoculated my imagination. I have had numerous experiences that would count as conversion, if they had actually converted me. I remember Robert Runcie celebrating a eucharist in Canterbury Cathedral, when it seemed quite irrelevant to ask if it was true: it was clearly something to be part of.

AT THE other end of the scale, a couple of fundamentalists who had given up their lives to working with junky prostitutes in a provincial town broke bread with a quiet prayer over a PVC tablecloth, and that worked, too. In Medjugorje, I got zapped by the Holy Spirit, and was for a while quite speechless with love for my fatuous and ignorant fellow pilgrims.

All this made me think that it did not matter whether I called myself a Christian, but the Lambeth Conference of 1998 made me resolve not to do so. It was a triumph of the bullies, of the self-important, the vain, and the thoughtlessly cruel. I may be a sinner, I thought, but I do not wish to be mistaken for a bishop.

But the New Atheist movement made it quite clear to me that I'm not one of them, either. I'd like to believe in an Anglican afterlife where Professor Dawkins and Lord Carey share a hot tub in hell. It will be only hot, not scalding, and the vaporous burblings of their self-satisfactions will continue for eternity. No one else will hear, and they will never notice. All will be happy.

None of this is terribly satisfying. It is natural to suppose that our philosophical conclusions are the distinctive marks of our moral, and intellectual excellence, but that doesn't work for me. I know Christians who are nicer, cleverer, braver and more honest that I am. I even know some who appear to have no difficulty in believing the whole thing backwards — and not all of them are Roman Catholic intellectuals.

But I still can't do it myself. So why worry? Why not see it all as non-sense? Because really it isn't all nonsense. As a friend of mine, a former missionary, said once: "It's about the thing that is true even if Christianity isn't true."

Christian language does things that no other use of language can. I can conclude only that God has called me to be an atheist.

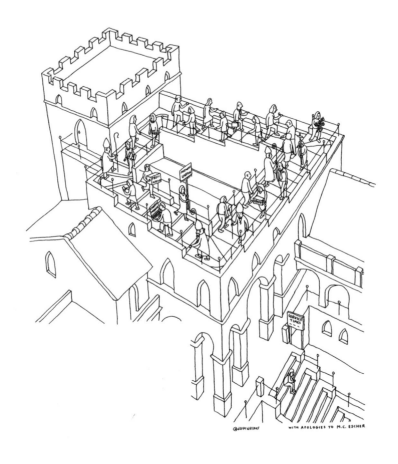

who's leading us, and where?

Not enough boots on the ground

The ranks of full-time, stipendiary clergy are ageing; the age profile of new recruits is older, and increasingly part-time. Soon, there will not be enough priests to go round, warns *Linda Woodhead*

ALTHOUGH the Roman Catholic Church has experienced a more dramatic collapse in the number of full-time stipendiary clergy, their numbers in the Church of England have also fallen. Until recently, however, the decline has been offset by a sharp rise in the number of clergy not paid by the Church, meaning that the problem has been masked — the overall number of licensed minsters has hardly declined at all.

Because this process has been gradual rather than planned, it has resulted in a proliferation of different categories of clergy and other types of minister. The Church's latest statistics on ministry begin with two pages of definitions of the various categories. Not all those who are ordained are licensed, but all those who are licensed (or have Permission To Officiate — whether lay or clerical) count as "ministers".

Leaving such complexities to one side, the overall result is that traditional full-time stipendiary clergy are now the exception rather than the rule. Today, there are more than 28,000 licensed ministers, of whom two-thirds receive no stipend. What the figures recently released by the Church's Statistics Department for the period 2002-2012 also suggest, however, is that this expedient can no longer cure the decline.

Between 2002 and 2012 the total number of full-time stipendiary clergy fell to 7674. The fall was greatest among men, and was partially offset by a rise in the number of female full-time stipendiary clergy to 1767 — an increase of about 40 per cent over the decade.

The growing number of ordained women has not been enough, however, to halt the overall decline of full-time stipendiary clergy. The decline has been compensated for by a growth in the number of parochial clergy working without a stipend, which rose sharply between 2002 and 2007, but has started to decline since then (to 3148). The fall in the number of Readers is particularly sharp: more than 20 per cent, over the decade, to 6623.

THE age profile of ministers suggests that 2002-12 represents a hinge period in the Church's history. Massive change was deferred by a volunteer army of people who stepped in to offer their services free of charge. They shored up the existing structure.

But that army is ageing, and moving towards retirement, and there are much smaller ranks of people — paid and unpaid — coming up behind. This is hardly surprising, given the general decline in Anglican affiliation and attendance.

Figure 1 shows that, like lay Anglicans, the majority of full-time stipendiary clergy are now aged over 50. The largest age group of stipendiary clergy — 42 per cent of the total — are in their 50s, and the average age of full-time stipendiary clergy is rising. In contrast, there are fewer than 100 full-time stipendiary clergy under the age of 30, and only one in five of them is a woman.

Women are concentrated in non-stipendiary ministry. Almost a quarter of stipendiary clergy are now female, and more than half of

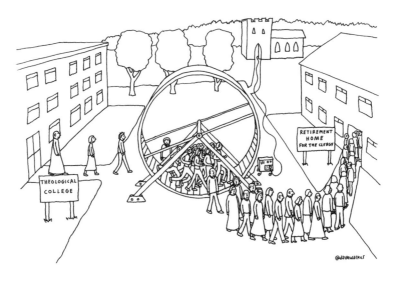

NSMs are female. Women now account for 16 per cent of incumbents, compared with seven per cent in 2002. But ordained women's age-profile is rising at the same rate as men's, with women's average age of 52 the same as men's.

The number of women under the age of 35 being ordained is tiny, and it seems that younger women are either not coming forward for ordination, or are not being recommended for training. In 2012, 71 per cent of candidates under the age of 40 who were recommended for training were male.

'Ministry in the Church has increasingly become a middle-aged or older person's calling'

The growth in the number of non-stipendiary clergy does nothing to alter the ageing profile of the clergy, because they tend to be even older than stipendiary clergy, who have an average age of 60. More than half of all NSMs and ordained local ministers (OLMs) are aged 60 or over, and of all non-stipendiary clergy, only three per cent are under 40, compared with 12 per cent of full-time stipendiary clergy. Similarly, 57 per cent of female Readers, and 61 per cent of male Readers are aged 60 or over; just two per cent of Readers are under the age of 40.

THE reality is that many of those who have been recruited and trained

FIGURE 1: AGE PROFILE OF FULL-TIME STIPENDIARY CLERGY 2012

AGE	MALE	FEMALE	MALE + FEMALE
UNDER 25	5	1	6
25-29	72	19	91
30-34	231	54	285
35-39	416	117	533
40-44	597	159	756
45-49	776	285	1061
50-54	1133	399	1532
55-59	1245	423	1668
60-64	1053	255	1308
65-69	347	53	400
70 AND OVER	32	2	34
ALL	5907	1767	7674

since the '80s are coming to ministry as a second or third career. They will exercise a correspondingly shorter spell of ministry. Although this brings the skills of mature people with a range of skills and experience into the Church's service, it does not help to recruit younger people.

Ministry in the Church has become increasingly a middle-aged or older person's calling, whereas the norm before was young men, often straight from university. "Now we have all grown old together, and simply recruited others of the same age or older," one incumbent, who was ordained in 1978, told me.

Figure 2 shows the breakdown of types of licensed ministers in the Church. Senior clergy make up about five per cent of all stipendiary clergy (this category includes bishops, archdeacons, deans, and other cathedral clergy; clergy working at Lambeth Palace are classified as extra-diocesan, and are not included in the statistics).

Of a total of 349 senior clergy in 2012, 39 were female, 24 more than in 2002. The average age of senior clergy is 52 — the same as other clergy. The average age of diocesan bishops is 62.

Chaplains account for five per cent of the ministerial pie. In 2012,

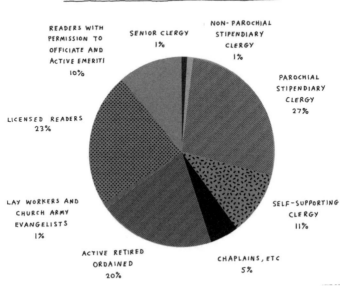

FIGURE 2: CHURCH OF ENGLAND LICENSED MINISTERS 2012

READERS WITH PERMISSION TO OFFICIATE AND ACTIVE EMERITI 10%

SENIOR CLERGY 1%

NON-PAROCHIAL STIPENDIARY CLERGY 1%

PAROCHIAL STIPENDIARY CLERGY 27%

LICENSED READERS 23%

LAY WORKERS AND CHURCH ARMY EVANGELISTS 1%

SELF-SUPPORTING CLERGY 11%

ACTIVE RETIRED ORDAINED 20%

CHAPLAINS, ETC 5%

there were 1018 chaplains, plus 315 non-stipendiary clergy, who work within dioceses but outside the parochial system, and 98 employed in theological and Bible colleges. This represents a decrease of seven per cent in the total number of chaplains over the decade. Army chaplains and hospital/health-care chaplains have experienced the larger decrease. A growing proportion of chaplains are female (241 in total).

THE number in religious orders is now small. It has fallen to 402 from 641 in 2002. The most marked decrease has been of professed lay women and female novices — there are currently seven female novices, and ten male novices. The number of Church Army evangelists has also fallen.

Although it offers only a snapshot, Figure 2 also helps us to see why the Church now faces a serious problem of staffing. It demonstrates clearly just how many ministers in the Church are now non-stipendiary: the two largest categories are Readers and active retired clergy. But of all types of ministers, it is these that are set to decline the fastest.

This is compounded by the fact that the loss of clergy significantly exceeds new recruitment. Retirements are high, and will continue to increase. The category labelled "Other losses" in the statistical tables is also very high. Indeed, in 2012, more clergy were "lost" (295, including 59 women) than retired (272). We do not know why so many clergy are leaving stipendiary ministry, or where they are going.

Ultimately, what the figures reveal is the end of a decade of respite for the Church of England — thanks to Anglicans' offering to minister without pay. This is a decade in which the Church could have been planning for the predictable changes that are now in train.

Put simply, the Church of England is soon going to have to operate with far fewer ministers, both stipendiary and non-stipendiary. Women's ordination has helped a little, but women continue to be disproportionately represented in unpaid, part-time, and low-status jobs in the Church. It is unlikely that this situation can be sustained — even if conscience allowed it.

To put it bluntly, there are no longer enough troupers left to keep the show on the road, and the show will have to change.

Listening out for the laity's voice

Lay people fund the Church, and run a great deal of its grassroots activities, but they are not sufficiently heard or recognised, maintains *Philip Giddings*

IN HIS introduction to *All Are Called* in 1985, Bishop Patrick Rodger wrote: "There are a great many laypeople, and clergy too, apart from those involved in Synods and PCCs, who want to find a voice in the Christian enterprise today. The best thing that our working party can do . . . is to leave some useful tools for the future thought and action of groups or individuals up and down the country."

Nearly 30 years on, it remains the ambition of many lay people to find that voice, and to play their part in the Church, of which they are numerically by far the dominant part. Much lip service has been paid to the notions of shared ministry, lay participation, the priesthood of all believers, every-member ministry. Much frustration, confusion, and unfulfilled potential remains.

All Are Called noted the progress that had been made in the previous 30 years, but frankly acknowledged the obstacles that continued to "hamper the development" of lay involvement.

It mentioned four: (1) the Church's "pitiful" and "grossly in-adequate" direct investment in lay education and development; (2) the neglect of the responsibilities of the laity outside parish life in the use of those funds that were made available; (3) a sense of oppression among laity — and clergy — from "persistent clericalism"; and (4) the ambiguity of the Church's understanding of where the local parish is valuable, and where it is not.

The report said that "Some clergy and parish lay workers forget that their fellow believers who minister mostly in the structures of the world may be just as committed to Jesus Christ, and just as faithful as they are themselves."

Many of the same points were made during the General Synod House of Laity's debate on lay discipleship in York last year.

Two things stood out. First, a great deal of ministry, witness, and

55

service is carried out by lay people in and outside the Church, much of it unacknowledged. Second, there is a great deal of untapped potential which, if mobilised, could transform the Church's apparent shortage of financial and human resources.

Yet there is no doubting that there has been a great flowering of ministry, and service, by lay people in the past 30 years. Many more lay people are contributing, both within the life of the Church and in the wider community.

'Some feel frustrated and unappreciated'

Youth work

THERE has been a much-needed growth of youth work: individual and groups of churches employ full-time and part-time workers — some ordained, but mostly lay people. There is a parallel, but not yet such substantial growth, in children's work (especially with toddlers), such as Messy Church.

Lay people are making a powerful contribution in the creativity, insights, and the models of discipleship that they provide.

Prayer ministry

THIS has seen considerable and varied growth. It was an unintended consequence of liturgical revision that intercessions in Sunday worship are led by lay people.

Alongside this is the wider availability of healing ministries and associated forms of prayer ministry. Here, a growing number of lay people — often in teams, and involving several local churches — are exercising their spirituals gifts for the church and the community.

This is increasingly linked with a ministry of hospitality and visiting, complementing established and more specialised ministries. The ministry of street pastors, which has grown significantly in the past ten years, also often contains an emphasis on offering prayer.

Home groups

THESE are a frequent feature of many parishes, providing fellowship, prayer, and opportunities for teaching and learning. In most cases, these groups are lay-led, and provide an opportunity for many lay people to develop their discipleship.

The use of small groups in evangelism often combines the hospitality and home-group culture. This, too, requires the essential leadership and participation of lay people.

The Alpha programme, for instance, has shown that this style of ministry can be effective in a wide variety of social contexts.

Schools ministry

A NOTABLE feature of the past 15 years has been the recovery of confidence in the Church's ministry in schools, which began with the Dearing report. While school chaplains make a vital contribution, the main task of providing a Christian presence in primary and secondary schools falls to lay people — particularly teaching staff, but also governors and, most importantly, the pupils themselves.

Here is the front line of the Church's engagement with the whole community. The only Christians whom most people under the age of 20 know are those they met at school. As a Church we have, at last, begun to wake up to the necessity of giving them the support they need.

UNFORTUNATELY, running parallel to that flowering of lay ministry and discipleship has been a decline in both attendance at church and the numbers of clergy.

Increasing costs mean that more and more will be required of the laity if the Church's ministry is to continue. The challenge is well-expressed in the three themes adopted by the national Church: contributing to the common good; going for growth; and reimagining ministry. All require a fundamental reassessment of our approach to the use of the gifts and insights of lay people.

Nowhere is this more evident than in the workplace. Here, too, there is at last a growing understanding of the significance of the part played by Christians, both in their work and in the way they conduct themselves.

One missed opportunity of the past 30 years has been to refresh and develop Reader ministry, and, in particular, to enhance its distinctively lay character. Consequently, the Reader profile is ageing, and recruitment is down.

A vigorous General Synod debate in 2006 led to the setting up of a review. The outcome, *Reader Upbeat*, was a disappointing, rambling report. The momentum was lost.

So, where are the laity? Many are hard at work sharing in, and resourcing, the Church's mission and ministry in the community and workplace, as well as in places of worship and committee rooms.

Some are frustrated, and feel unappreciated or marginalised. Some — perhaps many — could be inspired and equipped to do more.

Yes, all are called. The challenge is to release their energy and desire to serve; so that they may, in turn, inspire and equip others.

Clumsy, dysfunctional, and dangerous

The Church needs strong leadership. Instead, it is clumsy and ungovernable, says *Philip North*

FIGHTING and conflict were raging across Syria. In this country, hundreds of thousands of people on benefits were turning to foodbanks and loan sharks in order to feed their children; and clergy were coping with the harsh realities of ministry in a post-Christian culture. And what were we talking about in last November's sessions of General Synod? Ourselves, mostly.

In particular, we were discussing a motion from the London diocesan synod urging us to find a less "parliamentary" and more consensual way of making decisions — a motion that, unsurprisingly, was overwhelmingly rejected.

Of course, there is much more to our structures as a Church than the General Synod. But the existence of so self-obsessed and out-of-control an organisation at the heart of our life symbolises in so many ways the innate ungovernability of the Church of England.

The General Synod is more than just dysfunctional: it is dangerous. It is innately conflictual, its hallowed processes making no space for listening or genuine engagement. Its set-piece, pre-scripted speeches encourage the sort of grandstanding and attention-seeking which is inimical to proper decision-making.

It has, in abundance, the worst aspects of parliamentary-style democracy, but none of the traditions (party discipline, whipping, committees, etc.) which allow for the building of consensus and compromise.

It is disgracefully expensive. Its membership is all too often complacent, static, and bitterly resistant to reform or change. The car crash of November 2012, over women bishops, was inevitable, and it is only by interfering with due process — in a manner that the Church's civil servants are likely to resist ever happening again — that a way ahead appears to have been found.

AS ANGLICANS in the UK, we are looking down an evangelistic cliff of unimaginable depth. The demographic time-bomb, the triumph of secular materialism, and the post-modern distaste for religious institutions mean that no number of Messy Churches can hide the reality of the crisis that is approaching. At a time such as this, the Church needs strong leadership, clarity of vision, disciplined use of resources, and unity of purpose.

Unfortunately, as the General Synod so potently demonstrates, our clumsy structures render such things impossible. We may know what we want; but the problem is that the complex, inherited pattern of governance procedures, appointments processes, canons, laws, and traditions make it undeliverable.

Take, as another example, the bench of bishops. They are a highly committed and faithful group of men who work incredibly hard, and often under levels of stress that threaten their well-being. But they are lumbered with a job that is impossible. Their shiny new job descriptions give them terrifying responsibility for the mission of the Church across vast tracts of the nation, but they have hardly any levers of power with which to deliver on the expectations that we lay before them.

'Our inherited processes are unfit for purpose'

MAROONED in a sea of clergy conditions of service, private patronage, canon and charitable law, synodical muscle-flexing, opinionated archdeacons, and bossy diocesan secretaries, they have highly limited room to manoeuvre or bring about real change.

All they have left to resort to is the formation of well-intentioned, alliterative vision statements, or the privileged comfort of the House of Lords.

And, of course, a great deal of the problem lies with people like me. We parish priests do not especially want to be managed, governed, or led. In fact, avoiding such things was a factor that led many of us towards ordination in the first place.

There are many cases where the extraordinary freedoms allowed to parish priests lead directly to entrepreneurial and risk-taking ministry, and thriving local churches. But, equally, there are many others where it has resulted in inactivity, laziness, and death.

All the studies show us that quality of leadership is the biggest factor in enabling a Church to grow.

Bishops long to find ways of developing the capacity of their priests, and in things such as ministerial review and the Continuing Ministerial Education programme of in-service training they have some resources to offer. But the problem is that, unless those priests choose to co-operate, no one has the power to do anything about it.

THE results of this decision-making paralysis come home most clearly to me when it comes to church planting. Five years ago, an ordained friend, along with his small but wonderfully bold pastorate group, was asked to reopen a church building that had been made redundant some 20 years previously.

In order to achieve what the Bishop had asked him to do, the priest had to negotiate the project through six PCCs, deanery synod and chapter, the pastoral committee, the diocesan finance committee, the diocesan advisory committee, the Bishop's Council, and numerous consultative bodies.

There was £200,000 in inherited costs to be paid off, in addition to £150,000 for urgent, remedial repairs, and the new church had to guarantee financial viability from day one (including the payment of, in full, the priest's stipend and rent).

The whole process took more than three years, and included a number of setbacks that would have caused most mortals to give up. And this was in a diocese that is highly committed to church-planting.

It is no wonder that so many church-planters sidestep such arcane and dysfunctional processes, and simply get on with the job. For all the lovely language, our structures are as anti-evangelistic as ever.

It is easy to vent frustration by criticising individual leaders. But, actually, this doesn't help, because the problems are structural. Our inherited processes are unfit for purpose, and are incapable of delivering the "Church in mission" which we all want to see. We spend far too much of our time and energy having to manipulate, or fight against structures that should be there to assist us.

We can all dream of a new-look Church with clean, flat, transparent decision-making processes, strong and empowered leadership, and a reformed Synod working to help the local churches to flourish. The trouble is, someone will vote against it.

Far more likely is that we will have to allow the current broken structures to die, and enable something else to grow up from where the Church's heart and soul really lies — in the local.

Fresh ideas on leadership

Fresh expressions of church are multiplying, and their
numbers growing. They also feature different models of
leadership, reports *Graham Cray*

AS THE 12 years of my involvement with fresh expressions of church
have progressed, the issues of leadership, and the language of
"pioneering", have become increasingly central to my thinking and
concerns.

The Church Army's Research Unit study on fresh expressions in ten
dioceses reported that 21,000 people attended these new forms of
church — the equivalent of an additional medium-sized diocese. Some
42 per cent of these people had never been involved in a church
previously, and 44 per cent were under 16 years of age.

For every one person deployed by a parish or deanery to plant a
fresh expression, another 2.5 were added. This is good news, and it also
reveals a new pattern of leadership.

A total of 518 fresh expressions of church were identified on the
basis of a set of criteria which included the presence of "some form of
leadership recognised within and also without".

Just over half are lay-led, two out of three of these being women.
Two-thirds of the ordained leaders are men, who are more likely to be
full-time and paid than the women, who are more likely to be part-
time and voluntary.

Of the lay leaders, there is a growing proportion (almost 80 per
cent) of what the researchers call "lay lay leaders" — by which they
mean "people without formal licensing, and quite possibly without
designated training to lead a fresh expression of church, who
nevertheless are doing so, usually in their spare time".

Interestingly, exactly the same phenomenon is seen in the 2012
statistics of the Methodist Church, which has 46,000 attending fresh
expressions. The Fresh Expressions team is also aware of examples
where a fresh expression which was founded, or led by, a priest or
Church Army evangelist is now under able lay leadership.

Anyone exploring ordination in the Church of England, and who is seen as having a capacity for "oversight", is expected to have an ability to "pioneer". This is demonstrated by the many clergy who are also involved in starting and leading an impressive variety of models of fresh expression.

OVERALL, the Church of England needs and is developing — at least in part — a more mission-shaped entrepreneurial leadership.

The sheer number of "lay lay leaders" helps dispel a myth. Some parishes fear that planting a fresh expression of church will be one further demand on the same overworked volunteers. But the research reveals many new leaders who had not been energised by calls to staff existing programmes, but by these new missionary possibilities.

At St George's parish in Deal, a process of prayer and discernment led to the establishment of a range of missional communities. "One of the big things has been the whole release of leaders," the Associate Vicar said. "These people were sitting in the pews before, but now we have 40 missional leaders who are out there, leading."

There had been a hidden resource for leadership in mission, which was now being revealed. The evidence suggests that this could be true for many more parishes.

The Church Army research team excluded nearly half the examples considered, because they did not meet strict criteria. Some projects were primarily for existing churchpeople, while others were intended as a bridge to existing church rather than the planting of the new. The sheer scale of the other projects considered makes it likely that many more "lay lay" leaders are involved in them as well.

THE key to planting a fresh expression of church is close attention to culture and local context. It is the need to go and start the new, not just build bridges to the old, which has shown the need for a different "gift mix" for contemporary, missional leadership.

The inherited understanding of church, and church leadership, in the UK has never been static, but is substantially shaped by centuries of Christendom. Mission and ministry within an essentially Christian environment required pastor teachers much more than entrepreneurial missionaries.

The current context requires apostolic, prophetic, and evangelistic gifts, and reshapes expectations of the teaching and pastoral ones.

The Church has recognised this to a substantial degree, as seen in the way that the contemporary ministry context is described in the literature prepared for those exploring ordination, and in the selection criteria for Ordained Pioneer Ministers, and Church Army Evangelists. The gift is different because the ministry is different.

From one perspective, the responsibility being taken by "lay lay leaders" is relatively small. Most fresh expressions are planted by a team ranging in size from three to 30, and the average fresh expression has a "congregation" of 43 people.

The Church Army's quantitative research cannot provide full-blown, qualitative evidence of the depth of these new congregations, or the effectiveness of their leadership. But the indications are positive.

Thus, there is a whole body of new experience across the Church which needs to be harvested for the sake of those who will take up this challenge in the future.

Also, we need to take great care when attempting to offer training. An over-intellectualised training, delivered by those with no experience of this ministry, will do more harm than good.

'Lay leaders of fresh expressions need some form of recognition and accountability'

CANON George Lings and his team identified 21 different models of fresh expression, and some (Messy Church and Café Church, for example) have national networks, where resources and training can be found.

The research says that those who had training or prior relevant experience are more likely to see ongoing growth. To help with that, the Fresh Expressions website is a primary source of resources and guidance for good practice, while the report *Fresh Expressions in the Mission of the Church* recommended the "mission-shaped ministry" course as the best form of initial training.

The research also says that accompaniment, or consultancy, is the best form of support, but suspects that it is in short supply.

Lay leaders of fresh expressions need some form of recognition and accountability. One example is the diocese of Leicester's process of licensing lay pioneers in partnership with the Northampton Methodist District. Pioneers also need appropriate, continuing support.

Ordained pioneer ministers (OPMs) represent a small proportion of the leaders identified in the research, and this is a resource which the Church of England has not yet learned to deploy to its best advantage.

In addition to a more pioneering clergy, and many more "lay lay leaders", the Church of England needs those whose whole vocation is focused around the planting of the new, and the creation of new communities where none exist. Our nation will not be re-evangelised just by parishes reaching a little further into their communities, vital as this is.

It is not true that all clergy and lay leaders can be pioneers in this sense. The New Testament teaches that not all have the same gifts, and social science shows that not everyone can be entrepreneurial. All parishes, and clergy, need to encourage and support pioneering gifts when they see them.

Those with the ministry of oversight should never feel threatened by people who have different gifts, and who can do things that one particular parish priest cannot.

The emergence of new leaders, and new capacities for missional leadership on this scale, is a sign of hope for all the denominations participating in the fresh expressions movement.

Generation A — the dwindling force

Older women do a great deal more than keep the pews warm. They are are significant leaders in their churches, discovers *Abby Day*, and they are not being replaced

"IT'S like sex," the frail, white-haired woman told me as she poured my tea. Sex is something that is inherent, she explained carefully, like religion; it's something that we just know. "No one tells us how to do it, do they?" she asked, with a bright laugh.

I shook my head, shocked into silence. Although I have spent the past two years studying them, each conversation reveals another surprising quality of these unique Anglican women, members of what I call "Generation A", born in the 1920s and '30s, mothers of the baby-boomers, grandmothers and great-grandmothers of Generations X, Y, and Z.

These are the older women laity, often invisible and unacknowledged as they lead from the pews, who rarely have time to take tea and talk about sex because they are too busy hauling heavy boxes up and down church stairs for the jumble sale, or dusting and polishing, or organising the rota of duties. This may well be the final active generation of the Church of England — because their descendants are not replacing them.

In losing this generation, the Church will not just be losing numbers, but a kind of labour, leadership, and knowledge which has quietly kept churches going. This "pew power" is different from priestly leadership, but has been, I conclude, instrumental to church life.

TO GET to know them, I joined the congregation of a church, and, with the permission of clergy and laity, became involved in many aspects of church work led, and largely carried out, by Generation A.

After one year of that close involvement, I maintained my presence in that church while visiting others to check whether my emerging findings and themes were found elsewhere. Most churches were in the UK, two in Canada, and two (Episcopal) in the United States.

Congregations were deliberately selected as "mainstream" rather than Evangelical, and had a regular Sunday attendance of 25 to 50 people, mostly over 60 years of age, mostly women.

Through close observation, participation in their routines, and events, lengthy conversations, and formal interviews, I have formed three specific conclusions about what they do, why they do it, and why it matters.

FIRST, there is more to church attendance than Sunday services. The weekday morning prayer and holy communion services are largely attended by small groups of three to ten people, mostly Generation A.

Possibly more important is the widespread church initiative known variously as "church watch", or "church openings", led by Generation A. Their rota ensures that they sit in the church for a few hours on weekdays so that it can stay open for the general public.

A few tourists may come in to have a look, others might briefly say a prayer in a pew, or light a candle; but there is a core, I noticed, who regularly come for a chat. Most are not members of the congregation, but local people, who are recently bereaved, or struggling with alcohol or drug habits, and are semi-homeless. All are lonely. Inside, they find a calm face, a listening ear, and often a warm drink and a generously loaded plate of biscuits.

When I asked one Generation A-er if she ever talked to her visitors about religion, she pulled a horrified face. "Never!" Her part was to listen, and make people feel welcome and wanted. That was how she practised, not preached, her faith.

THE second form of pew power I discovered revolves around the social calendar. Where there is piety, there's a party, and where there's a party, there is food and drink. Like Jesus feeding the five thousand, there always seemed to be a bottle miraculously appearing from a shopping bag to be shared around the table.

These days, more is shop-bought than home-made as the women age, and have less energy to spend in front of their ovens, but the generosity fuelled by often meagre pensions is abundant: layers of sliced ham, coronation chicken, sausage rolls, smoked salmon on brown bread, quiches, cheese, and trifle.

The space will be decorated, and tables set, in themes of the season. There will be plenty of talking; a great deal of laughter; always a raffle; and with Generation A the last to leave after the washing up.

THIRD, Generation A organises, and leads, from the pews, to create belonging. The rota is a sacred text, published in a prominent place near the main doors, so that everyone on it is acknowledged, reminded, and held publicly accountable for church cleaning, church-opening, greeting, and flower-arranging. The names are mostly female, and mostly Generation A.

The effect is not only to keep the church building functioning, but the people involved and interdependent: each person has a duty, and a larger team, and a community to which they belong.

It is also a safety net, as the women look out for each other, and members of the congregation, enquiring after people's health, family, and work. These are small groups with strong networks, managed mainly by Generation A. They ensure that no one will be neglected or forgotten if they become ill, hospitalised, housebound, or otherwise in need.

'The generosity, fuelled by often meagre pensions, is abundant'

When Generation A departs, professional cleaners and florists may be contracted, and catering companies hired for the annual Christmas lunch, replacing pew power with professional power.

As the churches close more firmly on weekdays, not many people will notice, apart from a few lonely people. This is a unique space, open unconditionally to anyone.

More widely, when organisations lose their most loyal members they tend to decline quickly. Much as I probe these issues with Generation A, I cannot detect panic. They have seen worse, and survived. And what is the point of faith, if not to sustain hope in the face of futility? Priests may need to think quickly about how to replace that kind of leadership.

Do we have the right class of bishop?

Leslie Francis has made a study of the psychological profile of Church of England bishops. He examines, from a scientific perspective, what the Church of England requires of bishops, and sees how the people match up

THE starting point from which to grasp the Church of England's understanding of episcopacy is the 1662 Ordinal for the consecration of bishops. Those called to the office of bishop are called to "Government in the Church", and "to the Administration". They are required to:

- instruct the people,
- banish and drive away from the Church all erroneous and strange doctrine,
- maintain and set forward . . . quietness, love, and peace among all men; and such as be unquiet, disobedient, and criminous, within your diocese, correct and punish.

Psychological-type profiling recognises the qualities identified in 1662 as describing individuals who display the following preferences within the framework of psychological type theory: sensing (S), thinking (T), and judging (J).

At its core, psychological-type theory identifies four significant, deep-seated psychological differences. Each of these four differences is conceptualised as binary polar opposites (such as male and female).

The two orientations — extraversion (E), and introversion (I) — are concerned with the source of energy. Extraverts gain their energy from the outer world of people and things; introverts gain their energy from the inner world.

The two perceiving functions, sensing and intuition (N), are concerned with ways in which information is gathered: sensing types begin with the detailed information (facts), and build up to the bigger

SO, TELL ME ABOUT YOUR MOTHER CHURCH

picture; intuitive types begin with the bigger picture (theories), and draw in the details.

The two judging functions, thinking and feeling (F), are concerned with ways in which information is evaluated. Thinking types base judgement in the head, using objective and logical analysis. Feeling types base judgement in the heart, giving weight to the human subjectivity within the situation.

The two attitudes, judging and perceiving (P), are concerned with the way in which the outer world is operated. Judging types employ their preferred judging function (thinking or feeling) in the outer world, and model a structured external environment; perceiving types employ their preferred perceiving function (sensing or intuition) in the outer world, and model a flexible external environment.

Within this context the STJ profile provides a tight management structure in which precision is more important than vision, systems more important than people, and structure more important than flexibility.

THE more recent Ordinal for the consecration of bishops set out in *Common Worship* provides greater detail, and this detail reinforces the need for the STJ management style; but the added emphasis on the outgoing nature of the office promotes weighting in favour of extraverted leadership (ESTJ) over introverted leadership (INTJ).

The management style favouring J is understood by designations such as: principal ministers of word and sacrament; chief pastors.

The particular strengths of the SJ temperament are focused by requirements such as: be guardians of the faith; follow the rules; accept the discipline of this Church.

The particular strengths of the STJ style are drawn out by the following injunctions: offer to God your best powers of mind; teach the doctrine and refute error; confront injustice and work for righteousness.

The exclusive emphasis on the T disposition is, however, qualified in the *Common Worship* ordinal, and tempered by some appeal to F: be merciful but with firmness; minister discipline but with compassion; be gentle and merciful to those in need.

'The desired profile for bishops is Extraversion, Sensing, and Thinking. Most clergymen are the opposite'

The distinctive strengths of the E disposition may be preferred to effect the following tasks: leading God's people in mission; knowing their people and being known by them; make your home a place of hospitality and welcome.

THE contemporary Ordinal of the Church of England describes an office that draws on the strengths of the ESTJ profile.

The Church of England currently selects its bishops from among its male priests. So it is worth asking how well represented the ESTJ profile is within that pool. In 2007, a group of us (with Bishop Michael Whinney) published a profile on 626 Church of England clergymen. Then, in 2010, we published a profile on another group of 622 clergy. Both profiles were uncannily similar.

While the desired profile for bishops is Extraversion, Sensing, and Thinking, the majority of clergymen are the opposite: introverts, intuitive types, and feeling types. Only in terms of Judging does the desired profile for bishops reflect the pool of clergymen.

In a paper published in the *Journal of Beliefs and Values*, in 2013, Bishop Michael Whinney, Dr Mandy Robbins, and I described our attempt to offer a psychological profile of Church of England bishops.

We posted 258 questionnaires to serving and retired bishops, and got 168 back (a response rate of 65 per cent).

Our hypotheses were that the Church of England's selection process of bishops would be more likely to recognise the call of:

- extraverts;
- sensing types;
- thinking types;
- judging types.

Our first analysis compared all the bishops with our data on clergymen. Three of our hypotheses were confirmed. The proportions of extraverts, sensing types, and judging types were significantly higher among the sample of bishops than among the sample of clergymen. There was no significant difference, however, in the proportion of feeling types in the two groups.

Then we remembered that the Church of England has two primary types of bishops (diocesan and suffragan), and that different selection processes are involved. We divided our pool of bishops into two groups, and set these two types of bishops alongside the clergymen.

This time, the results were startling. Now we found that the pool of diocesan bishops contained a significantly higher proportion of thinking types than found among clergy in general. At the same time, the pool of suffragan bishops contained a significantly lower proportion of thinking types than found among clergymen in general. This scientific study of episcopacy leads to three main conclusions, and a challenge.

The first conclusion concerns the power of psychological-type theory to illuminate the psychological characteristics associated with those called to the office of diocesan bishop. For this office, the Church is appointing clergymen who prefer extraversion, sensing, thinking, and judging. These are individuals noted for good skills in managing systems, and who will safeguard the traditions and structures. They may not be so good at handling people, envisioning innovative developments, or embracing change. They may represent "a steady pair of hands" rather than visionary leadership.

The second conclusion concerns the power of psychological-type theory to illuminate the difference in the psychological characteristics of suffragan bishop and diocesan bishop. The main difference is between appointing the system-centred head to the diocesan post, and the person-centred heart to the suffragan post.

IN MANAGEMENT terms, it makes sense to seek the different skills of complementary personality types within the episcopal office within a diocese. Unless this strategy is made explicit, however, the strategy may seem to be unfair to those suffragan bishops who see their appointment as a stepping stone to diocesan responsibilities, but then subsequently are never appointed as a diocesan bishop.

Made explicit, however, this becomes a structural opportunity within the Church, by emphasising a career trajectory for suffragan bishops outside the expectation of a diocesan post.

The third conclusion concerns inviting the Church to consider accepting the routine application of psychological-type theory within its human resource strategy, and to do so for two reasons.

'It makes sense to seek the different skills of complementary personality types within the episcopal office'

First, the present study (and the wider research literature on which it builds) makes it plain that certain aspects of personnel selection involve implicit criteria that map, in predictable ways, on to the constructs proposed by psychological-type theory. To acknowledge this practice would lead to the creation of greater transparency.

Second, if the Church were to have a clear view of the characteristics needed for effective ministry and mission at different levels of its structure, psychological assessments could aid in the selection process.

This study of the psychological-type profile of bishops may also challenge the Church of England to pose this question: "As the Church of England selects the next generation of diocesan bishops, will the Church be best served by continuing to place confidence in the STJ profile, with its strong emphasis on preserving the traditions of the organisation?"

Might the Church be better served (in some dioceses at least) by, say, the ENFP profile of bishops who are equipped to function confidently with public visibility, to shape a vision for the future, to motivate the hearts of men and women to catch that vision, and to respond to the changing contours of a vision-led Church?

Episcopal leadership of this nature would be neither scary nor unpredictable, if supported and complemented by an ISTJ/ESTJ team equipped to maintain the essential diocesan infrastructure, including diocesan secretary, archdeacon, cathedral dean, accountant, and chair of the board of finance.

Some leaders are born, not made

The research undertaken by *David Voas* suggests a strong link between church growth and the priest's personality

AS PART of the Church of England's Church Growth Research Programme, we conducted a survey of 1700 churches and ordained ministers. The findings highlight the importance of particular leadership characteristics and strengths.

Less comfortably, it also suggests that these qualities are not easy to acquire. There are strong associations between growth and personality type, but none between growth and attendance on leadership courses.

This message may not be a surprise. A number of people commented to us that a newcomer's first contact is often with the priest; and it has to be positive. The personality of the priest is crucial to the experience people have at church. Of course, by no means everything comes down to personality, and different circumstances call for different types of people.

Younger clergy are more likely than their elders to report growth. Gender makes no difference in this respect, nor does ethnicity. Marital status is not associated with growth, but having children living at home is. Young clergy, with young families, have the edge in leading vital churches. They need some time, though: growth is associated with tenure in the post.

It is natural to suppose that "churchmanship" may be connected to growth or decline. Clergy were asked to place their theological orientation along three seven-point scales, running from Catholic to Evangelical, liberal to conservative, and from Charismatic to non-Charismatic.

The association between churchmanship and growth is not strong. Self-reported growth is associated with Evangelical and conservative, as well as Charismatic tendencies, but with the other two variables held constant, only the Charismatic dimension has an effect. Once other characteristics are taken into account, churchmanship is nearly always reduced to insignificance.

WITH the kind permission of Professor Leslie Francis, the survey included a battery of items for the Francis Personality Type Scales. Like the familiar Myers-Briggs system, these scales represent an attempt to apply the psychological-type theory rooted in the pioneering work of Carl Jung. There are four dimensions, identified by the letter in upper case: Extraversion or Introversion; Sensing or iNtuition; Thinking or Feeling; Judging or Perceiving.

The first two dimensions turn out to be relevant for growth, for reasons that may seem natural. Extraverts are energised by dealing with the outside world. Whereas Sensing individuals are methodical and rely on experience, N-type people (those who prefer to gain information in an intuitive way) trust inspiration; they are likely to focus on possibilities and the bigger picture.

Previous research suggests that Extravert and iNtuitive leaders are good at developing a vision, and goals for the future, and at training people for ministry and mission. Extraverts also have an advantage when it comes to converting others to the faith.

In contrast, Introverted leaders prefer to be involved with the sacraments and administering the parish; Sensing leaders are also orientated towards visiting, counselling, and helping people.

The data show a reasonably strong association between self-reported growth and "E" and "N". The combination of "E" and "N" is particularly effective.

We found that clergy with an "I" and "S" combination are three

'The association between churchmanship and growth is not strong'

times as likely to preside over decline as substantial growth; "E" and "N" clergy are twice as likely to experience substantial growth as decline. These links between clergy personality and growth are corroborated by results from a much larger sample of clergy of all denominations in Australia.

THE effectiveness of a leader is ultimately a matter of specific qualities or skills rather than personality itself. If personality has an effect on church growth, it is because the characteristics that matter (such as offering inspiration, for example) come, more or less naturally, to different types of people.

It should be said, though, that people are capable of performing in ways that may not come naturally to them. Many ordained ministers are highly versatile, and successfully deploy different traits in different roles. It is important to try to identify the key qualities, not least to decide whether they can be taught.

We asked clergy to assess themselves. "What do you see as your strengths?" "Some of your qualities will be more or less developed, either in relation to each other or relative to the characteristics of others. How would you rate yourself on each of the following attributes:

Empathising: sensing what other people are feeling; listening and counselling;

Speaking: being confident when giving a sermon or addressing a formal meeting;

Innovating: regularly coming up with new ways of doing things;

Connecting: spending time with people in the community and listening to their views;

Managing: creating good systems and providing clear expectations to lay leaders;

Envisioning: having a clear vision for the future and being focused on achieving it;

Persisting: finishing what you start, despite obstacles in the way;

Motivating: generating enthusiasm and inspiring people to action."

WHEN we take one characteristic at a time, "motivating", "envisioning", and "innovating" are strongly correlated with growth. "Speaking", "connecting", and "managing" are more weakly linked to growth, and "empathising", and "persisting" do not feature at all.

Two variables may be correlated, however, because each is also associated with something else. "Motivating" and "envisioning" remain important, positive qualities when controlling for other attributes.

In contrast, "innovating" and "connecting" fall short of statistical significance, and "managing" and "speaking" no longer have any real influence. "Persisting" and "empathising" now have negative effects — not, presumably, because these are bad qualities to have, but because these strengths are not congruent with flexibility and a willingness to push people in new directions. So, when we are examining what is conducive to growth, some qualities that would otherwise be strengths appear to be weaknesses.

More than half of the survey respondents had been on a leadership course, but this did not, of itself, appear to lead to growth. Perhaps there is an adverse selection effect (if people from declining churches are more likely to attend such courses), but it is hard not to be sceptical about the effectiveness of these courses in producing growth, however helpful they might be in other respects.

> 'Attendance on a leadership course did not, of itself, appear to lead to growth'

Serving the Church as an ordained minister is a vocation. All clergy have a calling. The question is: what, exactly, are they called to do? Not everyone is equally well suited to every task, and parish ministry involves many functions, from consoling individuals to inspiring whole congregations; from running the organisation to creating new forms of church.

To point out that people have different talents is not intended to make invidious distinctions. Generating numerical growth is an important objective for the Church, but it is far from being the only one.

A slightly disorganised religion

The Church has a great deal to learn from organisational theories, says *Margaret Harris*. Currently, there is a tendency to muddle through

DURING more than 30 years of researching with churches and charities, I have often seen clergy exhaust themselves trying to tackle practical challenges of organisation — challenges with which they are ill equipped to deal because they lack even rudimentary knowledge about the principles of organisational behaviour (OB).

Yet OB has heaps of intellectual tools to offer those running our churches. It could be usable knowledge, if more OB academics would take the time to adapt generic organisational knowledge to the special challenges that arise in faith organisations.

Meanwhile, clergy are left to muddle along as best they can, perhaps picking up bits and pieces of ideas from those books you find in airports that promise quick management fixes for businesses, or self-help secrets for ambitious careerists. It does not have to be like this.

There are ways in which individuals can draw useful insights from organisational disciplines without abandoning their theological grounding.

Let me outline some organisational insights that clergy and laity with whom I have worked have found useful. These are research findings from the OB field which can help to explain why things happen the way they do in churches, and so help leaders to devise sensitive and workable responses.

Implementation of change can be particularly intractable in association-like groupings such as parish churches. Since church adherence is essentially a voluntary commitment in modern Britain, authoritarian and prescriptive approaches to organisational change simply will not wash — irrespective of theological principles that give clergy the right to say how things should happen.

Anything — from changing the layout of chairs for meetings to implementing liturgy prescribed by bishops — can give rise to eruptions of protest from congregation members, and worse.

THE literature suggests ways in which such eruptions might be mitigated. They include developing a strategic plan over months, or even years, for staged or incremental change; informally involving key opinion-leaders in planning processes; and positively encouraging "pew-up" suggestions for changes, and their implementation.

More recently, church leaders have also found the so-called "theory of change" approach to be helpful. It suggests prior thinking about the precise nature of any prospective change; what the evidence of its implementation will be; and the rationale for taking a specific approach to achieving the desired endpoint.

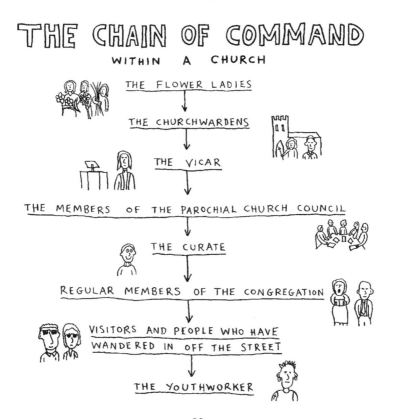

In adopting or adapting these kinds of ideas, church leaders might also take into account the special nature of goal-setting in a church context. Businesses, social enterprises, and even charities are free to take a broad scan of possibilities when making strategic decisions about their future aims.

But leaders in a faith organisation need to be constantly aware of what I call "low-goal ceilings". Clergy and lay people work with certain fixed institutional goals that — because they are part of the faith tradition — cannot be changed, or even debated.

'The organisational behaviour literature encourages us to step back, and ask what leadership actually means'

Clergy leaders are guardians of these fixed principles, and therefore have to hold a delicate balance between maintaining the distinctive faith "core", and having open and empathetic discussions with lay adherents.

The latter are demanded if change is ever to be achieved, but clergy have always to be aware of when a goal ceiling is being reached, and there is a threat to the very mission of the organisation.

A similar point can apply to the enthusiasm of visionary lay people who have new ideas for activities, projects, and fund-raising. It falls to clergy to ensure that innovation is encouraged while core religious principles are not infringed.

ANOTHER area of practical challenge for church leaders, where theology needs to be borne in mind, is organisational structure. Questions arise:

- Who has the authority to direct whom?
- Who is to be held to account when things go wrong?
- What should be delegated to committees, and working groups?
- Who can speak for the Church to the media? What roles can be shared between people, or across local churches?
- What is the appropriate relationship between local churches and their diocesan and national leaders?

It is often tempting to think that these kinds of questions can be settled by reference to religious prescription.

Yet apparent prescription may simply be "custom and practice" with a sacred aura. Even where there is clear religious guidance, there is often scope for adaptation to contemporary circumstances. All successful religious traditions have proved adaptable.

MOST people have some instinctive grasp of the working of "bureaucratic hierarchy" — one of the oldest of OB theories, which has its intellectual roots in advice given by Jethro to his son-in-law Moses, when the Israelite leader was trying to do too much alone.

Moses was reluctant to delegate his responsibilities, and Jethro told him how to construct a hierarchy that would spread the workload, but also ensure that final accountability for work done rested with Moses himself.

For a long time, bureaucratic hierarchy was pretty much the only organisational structural model around — adopted by firms, corporations, and armies, as a matter of course. Many religions, including the C of E, also adopted a form of hierarchy to administer themselves.

But more recent contributions from OB have suggested several alternative ways of structuring organisations — without hierarchy, or by using variations on the basic model: team-working between people with equal organisational authority; collective ownership structures; "flat" relationships between roles; leaders answerable to the members who elected them; and alliances between complementary organisations.

These are just a number of models, and they merit further exploration in the face of proliferating layers of bureaucracy and dwindling numbers of volunteer workers.

AS FOR the members and volunteers, who are the lifeblood of our churches, there is now a substantial body of research that offers sound principles for recruiting and supporting volunteers.

One of the primary principles is to work hard to find a match between the motives of an individual volunteer and the organisation's own needs. My own research suggests that clergy can be very good at discerning the varied and multiple motivations that people bring to church involvement, and at matching those motivations with church roles and tasks. They are also generally good at following another principle of volunteer management — thanking and recognising.

My final thought is about the very concept of "leadership". The Church seems to work on the assumption that its leaders are primarily clergy. The OB literature encourages us to step back, and ask what leadership actually means.

One answer is that a leader is someone who can nurture, inspire, and realise a vision. Visionary leadership, and the varied characteristics that encourage loyalty and inspire people to embrace change, is as vital for a religious organisation as any other.

So it is worth asking an open question about who may be able to exercise such leadership in the many and varied areas of church life. We need to cast the net as wide as possible — to catch laity as well as clergy, and fringe members as well as the most committed people who attend church.

**instruments
of change**

Measuring the Church's social footprint

Happily, Linda Woodhead finds that the Church of England also has a value and meaning for those who are not part of its regular congregations

LAST week, a young person asked me a question in response to recent articles in the *Church Times* which brought me up short: "What should change, Church or society?"

The reason I was dumbfounded was that I had never thought of the Church like that — as separate from society. The more I reflected on it, the less sense it made to think of a Church of England without England; it actually made more sense to think of a Church without congregations.

Imagine, for a moment, that all regular Sunday worshippers disappeared overnight, leaving only the clergy. Obviously there would be a financial crisis, the current parochial system would have to be radically reformed, a great number of churches and vicarages would need to be sold off, and the Synod would have to cease or change.

But the Church would remain, and its most influential activities could continue: occasional offices; Christmas services and other major festivals; cathedrals; civic and national rituals; chaplaincies; social action; schools; centralised church activities; bishops in Parliament; heritage sites; and the Church's living legacy of ethics and culture. Resources could be concentrated on them.

That is a fantasy, of course. But it is a way of making the point that an assessment of the Church's health has to do with more than just congregations. "Church growth" also needs to consider how well social activities are faring. Happily, the answer is not all doom and gloom.

MY SURVEYS last year found that half of all British adults (excluding Northern Ireland) reported having some contact with the Church over the past 12 months. And these numbers are not declining — those aged 18 to 24 report much the same level of contact as those aged over 60.

How do they connect with the Church? In descending order, the five most common points of contact are: funerals, visits to a cathedral or historic church, weddings, Christmas services, and christenings. Regular worship came in sixth place.

There is some variation by age. The top three for over-60s are funerals, regular worship services, cathedrals. For those aged 18 to 39 it is funerals, visiting cathedrals, and weddings. Not surprisingly, schools and school chaplains are also important points of contact for some younger people. More surprisingly, Christmas services are more popular with young people than older ones.

In the educational sector, we find obvious vitality. Church of England schools still play a vital part in the English education system, generally perform well, and are popular with parents. When asked why they would send a child to one, parents who completed our survey gave four main reasons: academic standards, location, discipline, and ethical values. These are traditional Anglican commitments.

Another area of societal Church which is doing well is cathedrals and heritage. The Church's own statistics reveal that, although Sunday worship is declining, interest in cathedrals — above all, midweek choral evensong — is going in the opposite direction.

@davewalker

There is also growing public interest in other activities that involve participation in history, such as choirs, pilgrimages, and Mystery plays. It is hardly necessary to mention cathedrals' and abbeys' continuing success in orchestrating national pageants, from funerals to royal weddings. Historic parish churches are also widely appreciated — just not for regular worship.

THE part played by the Church in social welfare is much harder to measure. Studies veer wildly from suggesting that the Church is in a position to take over welfare functions from the state to finding that its impact in even some of the most deprived areas of Britain is minimal or non-existent.

When I asked about contact with the Church over the past year, one per cent of the population reported having received help from the Church. As Professor Adam Dinham explains (*page 92*), the Church's mode of social action has changed, from leading projects nationally and locally to working in partnership with other faiths and statutory bodies. This is an inevitable consequence of congregational decline, and the growth of a multi-faith landscape.

But, of course, not all social action is carried out by congregational volunteers; lay-led, quasi-autonomous Anglican trusts and charitable bodies continue to make an important contribution.

When it comes to the Church's occasional offices of baptisms, weddings, and funerals, the picture is more easily quantifiable — and worrying. Even though they remain the Church's most significant points of contact with society, their popularity is waning.

It is not that people no longer want such rites — far from it. A re-ritualisation of personal life has been taking place since 2001, which has seen the rise of baby-naming ceremonies, school proms, engagements as a rite in themselves, more lavish weddings, divorce parties, marriage re-dedications, and so on.

Growing numbers of people, however, are doing these things outside the Church. Baptisms in the C of E have fallen from 20 per cent of live births in 2000 to 12 per cent in 2010. Funerals have dropped from 46 per cent of deaths in 2000 to 37 per cent in 2010. And, between 2010 and 2011 alone, the Churches of England and Wales conducted seven per cent fewer weddings.

THE Church's changing influence in the media, in civil debate, in value-change, and in political life are other important areas to consider, and they will be touched on in the final section of this book. Whatever detailed judgement we make, no one seriously maintains any longer that religion is becoming a purely private matter.

Overall, then, the report on the health of the societal Church must return a mixed verdict. Some parts look healthy; some do not. So, what makes the difference?

The single most significant factor seems to be a willingness to abandon a paternalistic mode of action. The bulk of the Church's social activities — and many congregational ones, too — were shaped in the 19th century in response to the demands of urban industrial modernity, and missionary activity. They were premised on social inequalities that were rarely challenged, and had to do with dispensing salvation goods, educational goods, and material goods to "God's children", and the "poor and needy".

Those forms of Christian activity which have not shaken off this paternalistic mode are in trouble. Where they have given way to genuine partnership, and co-creation, they tend to be doing much better.

It is the difference between asking parents to have their child baptised in a Sunday service, among people they do not know, and making the family the centre of the event. It is the contrast between designing a funeral with the active participation of the bereaved, and telling them that they cannot even have the music they want.

It is the shift from school chaplains who were there to give Christian "instruction" to the employment of chaplains — even in non-faith academies — to support the moral and general well-being of the whole institution. It is the difference between being a Church that works with other agents in society — and is open to being changed by them — to one that claims to be the sole repository of truth.

Rather than ignoring or repressing the Church of England's deep insertion into society, the time seems ripe for rediscovering it as its saving asset. My point about a Church without congregations is tongue-in-cheek. Success always depends, in part, on activists. But once the Church starts to exist for the benefit of activists alone, it ceases to be a Church, and becomes a sect.

Church for the nation, or national Church?

The C of E has a long history of social action, says *Adam Dinham*. How does this tie in with the state and other faiths?

A GREAT deal has been said about religion being back on the agenda, but faith-based social action has long stood proud in the landscape. A recent report by the think tank ResPublica singles out the Church of England as a body that is "delivering a greater level of care than the state and the market were ever able to do".

It thinks that the C of E has the "resources, experience, intention and will", and urges the Archbishop of Canterbury to "universalise Christian social action" as the main ambition of his primacy.

This is seductive. But it poses difficult questions for the Church of England's social action in a context where the landscape of religion and belief is not what it was the last time it called itself the national Church.

For governments across the West, the attraction is not beliefs and traditions themselves, but how they can be turned to the common good. As states roll back, they are well aware of the need to fill the gaps, and faith groups of all kinds have been seen increasingly as repositories of resources.

There is nothing new there. But in Britain there was an important turn in the 1940s, when two Williams — Temple, Archbishop of Canterbury from 1942-44, and Beveridge, his civil-servant friend from their Oxford and Settlement Movement days — thought welfare simply too important to leave to the well-meaning amateurs. They envisaged a welfare state — a phrase coined by Temple himself.

Much changed as a result. The transfer of welfare from Church to State undid centuries of paternalism, sexism, and top-down philanthropy which reeked of the *noblesse oblige* which the two great wars had done so much to undermine.

Care was now an entitlement, not a privilege. It also challenged the random nature of welfare provision. Until then, the parish you found yourself in would determine the quality and availability of services that you could draw on. Church-based social action had been the biggest postcode lottery of all. The State, on the other hand, would have the power and capacity to redistribute care, according to need.

THE reality of the welfare state has always been more mixed than it looked. It is clear that the State never did do it all. Church-based community work was especially active throughout the '50s, '60s, and '70s, and the tradition continues today.

More recently, various reports by faith groups claim a crucial contribution in countless social-action projects.

In the West Midlands, for example, *Believing in the Region* (2006) reported that 80 per cent of faith groups delivered some kind of social service to the wider community. In the North West, *Faith in England's North West* (2003) stated that faith communities were running more than 5000 social-action projects, generating an income of £69 million to £94 million a year.

In the New Labour years, this was especially encouraged, and policy coalesced around the government report *Face to Face and Side by Side: a framework for partnership in our multi-faith society*. But this promoted multifaith social action and dialogue, accompanied by national funding streams, as well as support for nine regional, multifaith forums. The vision was of a "multifaith society", echoing a multicultural one which had already long been promoted.

This reflected an understanding that things had changed since the Church of England could properly be called the national Church. Policy envisaged the repopulation of the now mixed economy of welfare — not with the well-meaning Anglicans of pre-1948 Britain, but with providers from the full plurality of religious traditions. Faith-based social action looked much more like the nation it served than the Church of England tends to on an average Sunday morning.

THE present Government has an anachronistic streak when it comes to religion. It observes, in the Church of England's parish system, a presence in every neighbourhood from which to reach across the whole range of traditions.

It wants the C of E to facilitate faith-based social action by all, for all. *Near Neighbours* is the Church's understandably enthusiastic response

— a C of E initiative delivered through the Church Urban Fund. It looks like a timely stream of funding from a well-established body.

But it also reflects this retrenchment to a Church of England lead. The programme places value on parishes as a primary source and focus, saying that: "*Near Neighbours* taps into the unique Church of England parish system, which has presence in all neighbourhoods and an ethos as the national Church with a responsibility towards all in the parish."

It says that "people of any faith will be able to bid for funding through the local parish church." The challenge for a multifaith Britain is that it depends on the parish system not only of a single faith, but a single denomination within that faith.

The risk is that a religiously diverse public sees this as a shift from a multifaith social action to one in which the Church of England acts as the gate-keeper, and is given value at the expense of minorities.

'We risk a return to random forms of top-down philanthropy'

This could undo a decade at least of relationship-building, and fails to make the most of the contributions that faith groups have already demonstrated. Coupled with the ideological withdrawal of the State, what is also risked is a return to random forms of top-down philanthropy, and paternalism, as wealthy individuals and churches give money according to unaccountable criteria of their own devising.

The Church of England has fewer — and older — people in the pews, and in the pulpits, who are not being replaced, and many parishes can barely afford to keep the roof on, and pay clergy pensions, let alone provide the repositories of social action which the Government expects.

Even if the old ladies could live for ever, and the money and structures were there to universalise Christian social action, as ResPublica imagines, a multifaith society is unlikely to welcome it.

The future lies in the Church of England's helping to hold open a space for faith-based social action, and participating alongside everyone else as their equal. It courts dissent at best, and irrelevance at worst when it attempts to lead the pack. The Church of England serves best as a Church for the nation, not as the national Church.

Public voices and private feelings

Anglican social thought is sprawling, unofficial, and incoherent. It is still evolving in response to changing circumstances, says *Anna Rowlands*

WHEN the newly elected Pope and the Archbishop of Canterbury met in Rome in the early summer of 2013, an unprecedented suggestion emerged. Why not work together to address the global issue of suffering and poverty? A mutual confidence in integrating evangelisation and social witness has been one of the most striking features of the early stages of both men's leadership.

And yet the critics have their questions. Laudable as the intentions may be, do we really need more church statements and episcopal initiatives on social issues?

Despite the surprisingly approving headlines, does this not sound like more of the wrong kind of Church paternalism? Isn't this too top-heavy when the energy should be going into a much more relational, and intensely local process of renewal? Is all this a distraction from the Church's setting its own house in order? Others wonder, when the bishops speak publicly on political and moral questions, who it is that they meaningfully represent.

The research conducted by Professor Linda Woodhead throws up two paradoxical realities. When the Church speaks on social issues it often does not represent the views of the laity. This is the social-values gap. Yet the findings also indicate that the Church continues to be valued for its willingness to raise ethical matters in public debate.

Our social values have changed in other ways, however, that are deeply relevant to the vocation of the Church of England, too. Earlier research has shown that our ideas about social duty and citizenship have been affected not just by the decline of religion, but also by in-dividualism and consumerism.

It is not that we now think less about social duty or the common good, but we do so in rather different terms. As individuals, our conception of the common good has mutated away from a strong focus on the nation or state towards a more fragmented identification with the global and the local.

WHILE the social tradition of the Church of England has always placed great emphasis on the local, it has also perceived its unique vocation to foster a Christian vision within a national community. To grasp this means taking in something of the long view.

Unlike its more formal cousin Roman Catholic social teaching, Anglican social thought is a sprawling, vibrant, and unofficial body of thought. The coherence of the Anglican social tradition does not lie in social principles or official statements. Indeed, the Church of England has historically sought to protect the laity from a teaching magisterium.

Rather, both Evangelical and Catholic traditions within the Church have placed strong biblical and doctrinal emphasis on the incarnation. Virtue was to be fostered through worship, and focused on real and practical expressions of fellowship and service.

In this context, the practical "social incarnationalism" of the 19th and 20th centuries emerged from quite different spiritual traditions within Anglicanism, each responding to their particular contexts. Innovations in schooling, nursing, home- and prison-visiting, and political campaigning were historically significant fruits of this plural labour.

But these were more than simply important social practices, inspired by the deep channels of spiritual life running through the Church of England. From Richard Hooker, through William Gladstone to William Temple, the mainstream Anglican social tradition has worked — and reworked — a distinctive Christian vision of a national society.

'The coherence of the Anglican social tradition does not lie in principles or official documents'

This vision was an ordered and hierarchical one. Christian citizenship was conceived in terms of a vision of a national Church, rooted through the parish system, and complemented by a limited but active state. A Christian religious presence was one of the basic conditions necessary for an active, free, socially just, and cohesive national life.

By dint of its vocation, it was the foundation of civil society. Our contribution to social institutions in the present time was connected to our ultimate citizenship in the heavenly city. Establishment, therefore, was less about the power and influence of the Church, and more a burden, borne gladly as a service to ensuring the best hope of a Christian politics, and a cohesive society. It certainly entailed privileges, but was primarily about responsibility.

IN HIS seminal work *Christianity and Social Order*, William Temple expressed this social Anglicanism in principles of "freedom", "fellowship", and "service". Temple argued for a collaborative approach to church-state relations, fostering new approaches to economics, education, welfare, and housing.

'Our notions of democracy, law and nationhood need to be renewed'

While not all of his theology has aged well, Temple's views have often been unfairly represented as narrowly statist. In fact, read carefully, it is clear that Temple was driven by a vision of the State in service to the vital life of local communities, fostering greater social equality, based on a sacramental view of human life.

The various church reports of the 20th century sought to bridge the local and the national through comment on perceived threats to the health of citizenship and social fellowship: debt and health, work, housing, education, and racism.

And these reports were, albeit unevenly, influential in public policy discussion. As late as 1997, at a time when a wider vision of full employment was lacking in economic and political circles, *Unemployment and the Future of Work* (briefly) received a serious hearing from the incoming New Labour government.

It is not just the ways that Anglicans were using the Bible to reach social conclusions that are important. What also matters is that the Established Church was interpreting its ecclesial task in a particular way. Threats to national unity were matters that touched on the core of Anglican purpose and identity — its ecclesial covenant with the nation.

Faith in the City arguably continues this focus, even though it was seen by some as a break with prior Anglican social tradition. Despite its embrace of liberation theology, the report remained centrally concerned with the character and cohesion of the national community. It simply brought liberation-theology perspectives to bear on that task.

The authors assert their Christian responsibility to speak from their local contexts, bringing to national attention the social realities they judged to threaten social integration: poverty, powerlessness, and economic inequality.

TODAY's Church stands on shakier ground, and it is the clergy in parishes and chaplaincies who are negotiating the complex faultlines that have emerged. *Unemployment and the Future of Work* (1997) was the last of the big commission-style reports, focused on Church, State, and nation.

A new generation of Anglican social theologians has welcomed the chance to think again about the covenant between Church and nation. When he was Archbishop, the Rt Revd Lord Williams began to frame the central question of Church and nation in a different way, raising questions about the shape of our economic life, militarism and nationalism, aggressive secularism, and inequality.

Much of what he said was premised on the importance of recognising that narrow ethnic and linguistic notions of national identity no longer work for us, and that our notions of democracy, law, and nationhood need to be renewed. All of this was part of the Anglican vocation to foster a covenant between Church and national community.

Migration, secularism, and interreligious realities were taken with absolute seriousness as stimuli to new forms of Anglican civic thought. As more aggressive forms of secularism challenged the very idea of a public Church, Lord Williams was left with little option but to venture newly angled ways to make the case for religion as itself a form of, and contributor to, public life.

Others have focused their vision of renewal more squarely on the local context. Professor Elaine Graham has called for the development of a renewed model of establishment "from below". She is one of a number of theologians who are calling for greater attention to the potential for interfaith partnerships and civic friendships that can arise and be nurtured best within the context of local faith communities.

FOR Canon Sam Wells, the answer seems to lie less in focusing on establishment per se, and more on rethinking our basic covenant theology. He sets a challenge to move from a logic of "working for" to a logic of "being with" others, at every level of church life. Dr Luke

Bretherton has pursued a study of the part played by the local church in community organising.

He suggests that local congregations, acting together with those of other faith traditions on the economic and social goods they share in common — such as a living wage, or action on payday lending — creates a new form of faithful social practice. For others, the answer lies in theologically infused attempts to recreate more participatory democratic practices: for example, through asset-based community development.

In their (very) different ways, these theologians are pushing less for a return to the era of Church statements and more to ways of reanimating the connection between various spiritual traditions within the Church of England and their social visions — encouraging these visions to take deep root in their contexts.

Perhaps, then, we can offer two-and-a-half cheers for ecumenical collaboration on social issues at the highest level. It is vital and exciting. But such statements will mean little if they happen in a vacuum. The reweaving of an Anglican covenant requires a rather deeper process of renewal.

Christianity — a cue for action

The Church has long been an engine for social activism, and continues to make a tangible impact, says *Stephen Timms*

IMAGINE, five years ago, that you were asked: "What would happen in Britain if hundreds of thousands of people were no longer able to afford enough food?" If it was me, I think I would have guessed that local councils would have organised something.

What has actually happened, however, is that the churches have stepped up to the plate. The Trussell Trust co-ordinates a fast-growing network, now numbering more than 400, of charitable foodbanks, all of which are church-based.

Three more open every week. They draw on charitable donations of food, and on large-scale volunteer effort. Between them, they provided food for more than half a million households between April — when the bedroom tax, and other benefit cuts kicked in — and December last year.

Most people think the churches in Britain are experiencing a slow but inexorable decline into irrelevance. The truth about Britain in 2014, however, is rather different. Only the churches have had the capacity to address a sudden crisis of food poverty.

And it is not just foodbanks. Debt advice, street pastors, helping jobless people into work, tackling homelessness, and international development: in all these areas — and many others — the churches are making a remarkable social impact.

We are seeing a new wave of church-based social activism. It is not just activism undertaken by people with a background in Christianity. Rather, it has the activity of worship right at its heart. This is what gives it energy and commitment.

THE number of people on the electoral registers of churches in the diocese of London fell sharply in the 20 years from 1972. But in 1992 the trend reversed. In the next 20 years, numbers climbed steeply — and, by 2012, they were back at 1972 levels, and still rising.

Immigration has been a big factor, and no doubt Alpha courses have played a part. But that numerical evidence — as well as reports of what is happening in communities across the country — suggest that the old assumption of declining social impact needs to be junked.

IN THE part of London I represent, London Citizens — a coalition of churches, mosques, schools, trade unions, and community organisations — has had a huge impact. It has enlisted young people to political campaigning far more effectively than the political parties did. It successfully recruited formerly unemployed people, many reached through their church or mosque, to work at the London 2012 Olympic and Paralympic Games. And it developed the idea of the living wage — an idea now taken up by politicians in every party.

Last year, I chaired the advisory committee for a study by the think tank Demos. Its conclusions were published last September, in *The*

THE CHURCH IS EMPTY

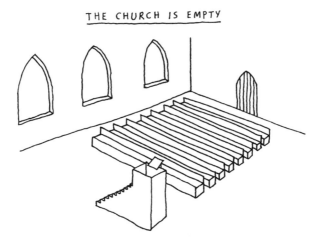

THIS IS BECAUSE EVERYONE IS BUSY

AT THE FOODBANK   AT THE YOUTH CLUB   WITH THE STREET PASTORS   AT THE DEBT ADVICE CENTRE

Faith Collection: Exploring the role of faith in British society and politics.

Drawing on data from the European Values Survey, it showed that people who said that they belonged to a religious organisation were far more likely to volunteer than people who did not.

In fact, the survey found that the one-in-eight of British respondents who said that they belonged to a religious organisation accounted for more volunteers with trade unions, in local community action, on women's issues, and on human rights and development than the seven-in-eight who did not. And the report points out that the political implications are far-reaching.

I chair the All-Party Parliamentary Group on Faith and Society. We have taken evidence from a wide range of faith-based organisations. Many of them report reluctance on the part of local authorities to commission public services from organisations such as theirs. In our view, this reluctance is misplaced.

'People who belong to a religious organisation are far more likely to volunteer than people who don't'

CONSEQUENTLY, we have drawn up a draft "covenant", comprising commitments to be signed up to by both local authorities and by faith-based organisations that are seeking local-authority contracts.

We hope that it will help to address the current reluctance. Local authorities recognise that austerity will require radical new ways of meeting needs in their communities. A few forward-thinking councils see partnership with faith groups as a promising option. We are discussing pilots of our covenant with a couple of city councils.

Of course, by some yardsticks, the social impact of the Church is much less than in the past. Its impact on public policy is slight — church opposition to the Prime Minister's Marriage (Same-Sex Couples) Bill appeared to have minimal effect on the public debate. Many people have no idea what happens inside churches — and no inclination to find out, either.

But popular respect for the Church, however ill-informed, has been maintained. In disadvantaged neighbourhoods, where many institutions have pulled out, the Church is sometimes the only one left. In those situations, it represents hope.

In previous centuries, waves of church-based social activism have had profound and lasting effects on Britain. They have delivered social progress. They have forged new forms of social organisation, and enduring institutions. It is too early to judge the long-term effects of this current wave, but the scale of it suggests that the effect will be substantial.

Living in an old country

Malcolm Brown believes that the relationship between Church and State reflects a deeply embedded Anglican Christian identity

"TO BE sure, if I was trying to get there I wouldn't be starting from here," the old Irish joke has it. If the UK was a newly created state, writing a constitution on a blank sheet of paper, how might religious belief be factored in to national institutions, national identity, and cultural life?

Probably not through the presence of 26 bishops of an Established Church sitting in Parliament, or through an MP's answering questions in the Commons about church affairs (or, rather, the affairs of one particular Church). Perhaps there would be no place in the fabric of the nation for religion at all.

But that is not where we are starting from. We started a long way back. We are, as the commentator Patrick Wright put it in 1985, "living in an old country". You do not have to know much history to sense that this is a country where history constantly challenges neatness and pure logic. Institutions and ways of thinking have evolved, changed, adapted, and grown to be what they are today.

There have been bishops in Parliament from its foundation, but the relationship between Church and State is not a matter of special privileges granted by an all-powerful State to one particular faith. It is a relationship that has been at the heart of our forms of government for many centuries, and which has weathered enormous changes — even a civil war.

That does not answer the question how things ought to be today. In discussing constitutions, government, and democracy, the constitutional separation of Church and State in the United States is widely thought of as somehow more natural, fair, and modern than the complex relationships still current in England.

But instead of the common assumption that "ancient" equals "anachronistic and pointless", a more useful debate would consider how far assumptions from a young country apply in an old country such as ours.

BISHOPS IN THE HOUSE OF LORDS

THEIR ROLES

SITTING IN THE HOUSE
(THEY TAKE IT IN TURNS)

PARTICIPATING IN THE
DEBATES, VOTING, ETC

STAYING INFORMED ABOUT
DIFFERENT TOPICS

HAVING A CHAT WITH MINISTERS

IT IS possible to defend some old institutions on grounds of utility. Along with the crossbench peers, the Lords Spiritual bring an important non-party dimension to the Lords' work of scrutinising and revising legislation.

The House of Lords combines members with party affiliations with those chosen for particular expertise, or who represent aspects of national life. Whether that balance is right is another matter, but the Lords Spiritual contribute two important things.

First, as diocesan bishops, they have a ministry and concern that is focused on a specific part of the country. They can speak for the communities of their dioceses with the authority of a Church that is present in every parish.

Second, they witness to the fact that we are not, in fact, a secular state. And this takes us beyond utility to consider matters of identity, and gets to the heart of our national difficulty in handling diversities of all kinds.

Behind the view that diversity necessitates an entirely secular state, which shows no overt allegiance to any faith at all, lies the odd idea that it is possible to adjudicate between diverse, and potentially conflicting world-views without having a world-view of one's own.

Tensions in the US between Church and State suggest that such neutrality may be hard to maintain. Completely separating religion from the State misses something about the beliefs that motivate people to commit themselves to the shared project that is the State itself.

Opening the benches to all faith communities raises problems, too. What counts as a faith? How should proportionality be handled? It is worth noting that other religious communities do not all think and behave in the way that the secularist mind might expect.

Few of the great world faiths in the UK would object to stronger parliamentary representation. But that does not mean that they all resent or oppose the particular part played by the Church of England, as several made clear in their formal responses to the committee examining the last Bill on Lords reform.

AS THE Queen said, in a speech to faith leaders at Lambeth Palace in 2012, "The concept of our Established Church is occasionally misunderstood, and, I believe, commonly under-appreciated. Its role is not to defend Anglicanism to the exclusion of other religions. Instead, the Church has a duty to protect the free practice of all faiths in this country. . . Gently and assuredly, the Church of England has created an environment for other faith communities — and, indeed, people of no faith to live freely."

'Separating religion from the State misses something about the beliefs that motivate people to commit themselves to the State itself'

If we fulfil that vocation, even imperfectly, many apparently anachronistic institutions, such as bishops in the Lords, the interweaving of canon law and statute law, and so on, begin to make sense. This is not, perhaps, in the strictly utilitarian terms of secular ideology, but in the context of an old country which tries to adapt its institutions to changing circumstances rather than wants everything to be logical, predictable, and subject to only one mode of temporal power.

Against that background, how is the Church of England doing today? In the Lords, there is a bishop on duty every day that the House is sitting. The idea that, day by day, 26 prelates sit in lawn sleeves and serried ranks, dutifully traipsing through the voting lobbies, is wide of the mark.

The bishops all have plenty to do in their dioceses. So it falls to one or two bishops to cover the enormously varied business of each parliamentary day.

They work in clusters around particular areas of interest — rural matters, the economy, health care, international affairs — with two or three bishops staying abreast of developments in each area. That way, there is a fighting chance that a bishop who knows a good deal about a subject can be in the House when that subject arises in debate.

'Britain's old institutions have not yet been eclipsed'

THE Lords Spiritual are backed up by the Parliamentary Unit, established in 2008, which is located in the Mission and Public Affairs (MPA) Division at Church House. Supported in turn by MPA's small team of specialist advisers, the Education Division, and others, the unit ensures that bishops are well briefed to contribute to debate.

The bishops do not confine their activities to the floor of the chamber: for instance, they may meet ministers to discuss government plans at various stages of the parliamentary process. That helps the Church to be well-informed as well as communicating its priorities.

Some serve on parliamentary committees, as the Archbishop of Canterbury did so effectively on the Commission on Banking Standards. That example shows how the Church's activity in Parliament spills over into its wider public position — and its daily life in the parishes and dioceses.

Archbishop Welby's work on the Commission on Banking Standards prompted his analysis of the financial crisis as a market failure. From that analysis came his interest in credit unions as part of the solution to the dysfunctions of the sector, leading to his creation of a task group to promote change in the industry, and to a grass-roots campaign to link the resources of parishes to their local credit unions.

One case-study like that is worth any number of lists to show how the Church of England in Parliament connects both to the "principalities and powers" of national life, and to the everyday existence of communities in cities, towns, and villages across the country.

A Church in an old country must be adaptable. The part it plays extends beyond the "anachronistic" Lords into the much more "modern" institution of the Commons. The Second Church Estates Commissioner is a member of the government of the day, who fields questions each month on matters pertaining to the Church of England.

HON. members are not only skilled in spotting the points where the life of the Church connects with the lives of their constituencies; their questions also suggest that what goes on in the church matters widely. They care about the culture and flourishing of the nation, and they see that the Church makes a difference to those things.

The Parliamentary Unit supports the Second Church Estates Commissioner, Sir Tony Baldry, as robustly as it supports the Lords Spiritual; and the range of topics dealt with in a parliamentary session — bats in belfries, same-sex marriage, women in the episcopate, the affairs of local churches, the policies of dioceses — are certainly stretching.

If you want to evaluate the impact of the Church of England on national life today, you could try to count person-hours given in service, church halls in community use, projects to alleviate poverty, and so on. It would add up to a great deal.

I prefer something less starkly utilitarian: starting with the deep embeddedness of Christian faith — and Anglican identity — in the history of the country, and the way we still understand ourselves as communities and as a nation.

It is impossible to quantify in statistics. But if you look, you will see it. And it reaches from the red and green leather benches at Westminster through to the battered pew of the parish church, and beyond that to the simple neighbourliness of Christian people in their communities.

I believe that old institutions in the UK have not yet been completely eclipsed, except in the rhetoric of those with an interest in eclipsing them. You would not invent it all to be like this. But, as we've got it, it is worth valuing.

A golden age for church schools?

The C of E was once accused of being embarrassed about its schools. They are regarded highly now by parents and professionals, reports Dennis Richards

IF ASKED which individuals have done most to "trigger" the transformation in the fortunes of Church of England schools in recent years, the names George Carey and David Blunkett might not easily spring to mind.

When Dr Carey, newly installed as Archbishop of Canterbury, asked a typically trenchant question of an audience of head teachers of Anglican schools, more than 20 years ago, he cannot have imagined where it would lead: "Why is the Church of England so embarrassed about its schools?"

The Archbishop was speaking against the backdrop of the opening stages of "the long goodbye". Local education authorities, the dominant force in English education for at least a century, were increasingly coming under sustained attack.

Successive governments, anxious to be in the vanguard of reforming what they considered to be a failed system, had begun to see the LEAs as dinosaurs of a bygone age, dedicated to preserving their fiefdoms and frustrating any move to change the status quo.

Ken Baker's city technology colleges, and John Major's grant-maintained schools cascaded into the torrent of Tony Blair's revolution. Specialist schools were followed by beacon schools. And there were indications that sponsored academies would become the mechanism of choice, to free schools of LEA control and lead us to the new Jerusalem. Michael Gove's free schools have surely completed the process.

David Blunkett, the long-time left-leaning leader of Sheffield City Council — at one time known as "the People's Republic of South Yorkshire" — stunned the Educational establishment, in 2000, with his extraordinary endorsement of church schools during his tenure as Education Secretary.

Famously stating that he would like to "bottle" the ethos of church schools and "spread it" round the system, he opened the door to a new era for church secondary schools.

THE Dearing report, driven by the leadership of Canon John Hall, the then general secretary of the National Society and now Dean of Westminster, set the agenda.

The Chadwick report, in 2012, gives a picture of the dramatic changes over little more than a decade. With 4800 schools in the "family", the Church of England is the largest single provider in England. One million children attend church schools.

Eighty sponsored academies, and 277 "converter academies" illustrate the extent to which the Church of England has embraced the new dynamic for educational change.

The Church of England can reflect, with some satisfaction, that the "new" academy provision is overwhelmingly in areas of high social disadvantage; that average free-school-meals eligibility is now 15 per cent (as it is in non-church schools); and that 25 per cent of the students are from black and minority ethnic backgrounds — almost identical to the proportion in other parts of the sector.

It would be wrong, however, to assume that all is changed. On the contrary, the primary sector remains much as it was. There are 4443 C of E primary schools, filling a position in the state sector established for them by R. A. Butler's great Education Act of 1944.

The so-called dual system is a model that has stood the test of time. Not only does the system involve Church and State on a national scale: it does so in microcosm in hundreds of small, often rural communities across the land, from Cornwall to Cumbria, where the village school has a Church of England foundation.

It is remarkable how successful the partnership has been. Such schools, for the most part, continue to function under LEA control and supervision. Considering themselves too small to choose stand-alone academy status, the multi-academy-trust model is in place to supervise schools that have "failed" an OFSTED inspection, and which the Government has compelled to leave LEA control.

ALL schools are now part of a "diversity and choice" system; so there is no longer any need to be defensive about the distinctiveness and proven success of Church of England schools.

A church-school expert, Professor Jeff Astley, has suggested that there are three considerations: education into Christianity; education about Christianity; and education in a Christian manner.

All state schools can aspire to the third. There will be little that is distinctively Christian about them. Roman Catholic (and Muslim) schools will unequivocally subscribe to the first, subject as they are to direction from their supervising bodies.

Church of England schools can afford to be altogether subtler, more responsive to a variety of local circumstances, and distinctive in a way which responds to Lord Runcie's words: we are "to nourish those of the faith, encourage those of other faiths, and challenge those of no faith".

There will be "no apology for theology", because RE will be of both high quality and high status as we pass on to our students a distinctive view of the Christian heritage and its contemporary challenge. We may even gently try to educate our students into Christianity in collective worship, mindful also of Lady Runcie's famous words: "Too much religion makes me go off pop."

> 'Most C of E secondary schools are rated "good" or "outstanding"'

This may be something of a golden age for Church of England schools. Subjected to the state's rigorous inspection regime, we know that 76 per cent of Church of England secondary schools are currently rated "good" or "outstanding" — above the proportion in other parts of the sector.

Accusations that Church of England schools favour the middle classes are withering on the vine, as huge numbers of disadvantaged students increasingly come under the Church's umbrella. C of E academies that are fortunate enough to be in the leafy suburbs, with privileged intakes, must now face up to the new challenge of joining multi-academy trusts with other church schools in radically different circumstances.

The gospel demands no less. It is an inspiring agenda. "Why is the Church of England embarrassed about its schools?" You must be joking.

More about solidarity than charity

Loretta Minghella applauds the Church's record in
supporting people in the developing world, and warns
against voices telling us that charity begins at home

EVER since the Middle Ages, when they were known for offering sanctuary to those in dire straits, churches have had a proud record of responding to human suffering. For many of us, the recent positive press highlighting the many food banks in the UK run by churches was welcome, but nothing we did not know already.

Whether it is running food banks, or night shelters, or raising money for people caught up in disasters such as Typhoon Haiyan in the Philippines, Christians are often the first to offer help.

Christian Aid, the organisation for which I work, is a living testament to that generosity. It was established in 1945 by the Churches of Britain and Ireland to respond to the huge suffering caused in Europe by the Second World War.

In an inspiring act of witness every May, Christians across Britain and Ireland take to the streets in the name of their faith to raise money for the world's poorest people during Christian Aid Week. The contributions of hundreds of thousands of supporters over many decades have enabled Christian Aid, working with partners around the world, to make deep inroads into the challenges of poverty in some of the most fragile and desperate places on earth.

I give thanks for the strong messages coming from church leaders, who continue to emphasise the need for Christians to make the concerns of poor people a priority. Indeed, as an ecumenical agency we are encouraged by what seems to be a renewed energy across the denominations for engagement on issues of poverty and social justice.

POPE FRANCIS has made headlines around the world with his fresh articulation of Roman Catholic social teaching. I was moved by the words of the Archbishop of Canterbury at last November's World Council of Churches' gathering in Busan, South Korea: "The true children of Christ act instinctively to love those who suffer, as he loves us. If justice fades, hope faints. But when justice is loved, and lived, the poor have hope, and the whole world begins to sing."

Speaking on her recent visit to London, the Moderator of the General Assembly of the Church of Scotland, the Rt Revd Lorna Hood, put it this way: "A bias to the poor is what the Church of Scotland sees as a priority in its life and mission."

'When Jesus called us to love our neighbours, he didn't have postcodes in mind'

For me, these messages speak to more than acts of charity in the sense of alleviating the symptoms of poverty. They speak to our calling to act in solidarity with those in poverty, and so to look for permanent solutions to the marginalisation and deprivation they face.

HERE is where I think we still have more to do together, to live out our Christian calling. We need to challenge and secure change to the systems and structures that keep people poor. I understand that clergy and congregations are besieged with causes, and, with campaigning, the journey can be long and uncertain, but no one said following Jesus was going to be easy.

I can see, too, why Churches often steer clear of potentially divisive party politics, but being "political", in general terms, is an important part of contributing to a healthy society.

Christians have a great deal to offer the political discourse, and I fear that we let down those in need when we vacate that space and leave it only to secular voices. When I found my faith again in 2002, I, too, thought politics was something better dealt with outside church. I was one of those people whom Archbishop Desmond Tutu was talking about when he said: "To those people who say the Bible is not political, I have to say, what Bible are you reading?"

It is safer and easier for us to keep our heads down, and not draw flak for speaking uncomfortable truth to power. But that did not stop Jesus from being overtly political. As well as being the Son of God, he was a radical activist, who challenged the powerful status quo of his time. He turned over the moneylenders' tables in the Temple, he preached good news to the poor, and he had a message of love so threatening to the powerful élite that they felt compelled to have him executed.

We have seen what can be achieved when churches come together.

Christians here were crucial in the fight against apartheid. In the United States, led by Martin Luther King, they played a significant part in the civil-rights movement. More recently, we had the Jubilee Debt Campaign, which has led to $130 billion in debt cancellation.

THERE are still some big issues that need the prophetic voice of the Church. Climate change is a scourge for many of the world's poorest people. Unscrupulous companies get rich from working in poor countries, yet fail to pay their fair share of tax in return.

We can be the voice of the voiceless and speak up on these issues in a way that gives politicians the encouragement and pressure they need to take the long-term view that is best for all God's people, not just some of them.

It might not be well reported, but many Christians are actively engaged in campaigning in this way. But there is more we can and should do. Archbishop Welby again: "When I read my Bible, I find that Jesus commands me to be very outspoken about the pressures on the poor." Although it can feel uncomfortable at times, I believe that challenging the powerful is one of the most effective acts of Christian witness.

A final thought: I am increasingly uncomfortable with the competition between the needs of people here in the UK and those overseas, and between those alive today and those yet to be born.

"Charity begins at home" is a cliché used to prioritise the needs of people here. But when Jesus called us to love our neighbours, I think we can be confident that he did not have any postcodes in mind.

I believe that we are called into right relationship with all people, God's image being present in everyone — North and South, today and tomorrow. And when we and our own country have had a hand in causing the problems affecting those far off, such as climate change, then we should be part of the solution.

Christians are increasingly seen as out of touch and divided over issues of sex and sexuality. We need to show the world another perspective. In the next couple of years, we face opportunities where the Christian voice on global suffering and poverty has to be heard: in the European elections, in crucial meetings to agree global strategies to tackle climate change, and, of course, the Westminster elections.

When we speak out on suffering and poverty — whether at home or overseas — then we will show God's love to the world.

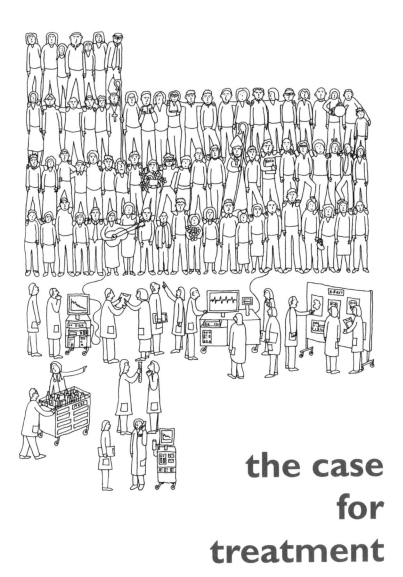

the case
for
treatment

A remedy for an ailing Church

The best way for the Church of England to keep body and soul together is to break itself up into a series of 'franchises', says *Linda Woodhead*

THE three parts of this book that precede this one make grim reading. The Church is sick. It is no good saying that God will save it, unless you are more convinced than I am that divine plans factor-in the continued existence of the Church of England. It is safer to listen to St Paul: God gives the growth, but a Paul has to plant, and an Apollos has to water. So what's to do?

We should begin by setting out the Church's problems in the context of wider changes that have taken place in the global religious landscape since the 1980s — above all, the emergence of a new kind of diversity within religious traditions which has an increasingly global and non-clerical basis.

In the C of E, for example, divisions between Low and High church parties — with clerical leaderships — have diminished as divisions between Charismatic Evangelicals, conservative Evangelicals, and various forms of liberalism have increased.

These identities are now global, as well as national and denominational. For example, Anglican Charismatic Christians often have closer links with born-again Christians in similar Churches around the globe than they do with fellow Anglicans.

Related to this is a struggle for the soul of all the main religions — especially Christianity, Judaism, and Islam. The battle is between "fundamentalists" and "liberals", who differ profoundly about the nature of truth, each believing that they are right and the other is wrong. In Islam, for example, the liberal Dr Khaled Abou El Fadl speaks of what he describes as a fundamentalist or neo-puritan "great theft" of Islam's soul.

It is within this context that we must view what has been happening to the C of E since the late '80s. A neo-puritan takeover is in process, despite the fact that not as many as one in ten Anglicans is aligned with this identity.

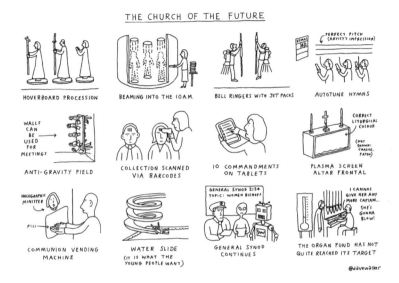

THIS explains why many Anglicans have come to feel unchurched by their own Church; why the Church is increasingly at odds with its society; and why energy has been diverted from everything else, including urgent structural reform.

One of the reasons why the C of E has offered little resistance to this narrowing of its profile is its leaders' devotion to unity at almost any cost. Bearing in mind the Church's historic commitment to "uniformity", this is understandable, even laudable. But it has had the opposite effect it intended: it has bought unity at the price of historic breadth and variety.

Let us not kid ourselves: the C of E is not one big happy family at the moment — it is an extremely dysfunctional one. Plenty of its members abjure one another. The situation has been made infinitely worse by the fact that they have been forced to live in closest communion, and play a zero-sum game, in which only one party can win.

The most realistic way of saving this family is by pursuing an amicable separation. Not divorce, not schism, but "facilitated separation", to coin a phrase. The fact that no other Christian Church has found a way of being genuinely pluralistic only makes it more important for the C of E to become a beacon in a world that is struggling to find constructive ways of coping with religious diversity.

IF THE Church is to go from zero to hero like this, a good way to do it is to rethink itself as a sort of religious franchise. Its various branches would retain loyalty to the C of E "brand" (after all, we already have a logo), and central services.

But the branches would have considerable independence, and be free to express English Anglicanism in ways that allow their distinctive forms of theological and ecclesiastical integrity to flourish.

IF WE time-travel to 2035, we can take a glimpse at this renewed Church, and its six distinct branches. Here is what they look like:

1. THE CATHEDRAL GROUP
"Celebrating the beauty of holiness since 597"

This is the chosen home for many historic abbeys, chapels, retreats, and churches — all of which unite around shared commitment to history, beauty, and ritual. This branch is flourishing: areas such as bespoke weddings, funerals, festivals, arts events, and national rituals are all in demand. It also makes money as an international consultant for large ritual events.

2. THE HEART OF ENGLAND GROUP
"The heart of the local community"

Many rural congregations opted to join this branch, along with some urban ones. They have turned churches and halls into welcoming spaces for everyone, and host all sort of activities, from Messy Church to creative-writing groups. Many are now lay-led.

3. THE ALPHA GROUP
"Freely exploring discipleship"

This is the umbrella for congregations of a Charismatic Evangelical hue. Its genius for organisation, professional management, and innovative teaching products, combined with its offer of personal growth through discipleship, has allowed it to consolidate and expand effectively, and it has established a significant international presence.

4. FAITH FIRST
"Strengthening the faith"

This part of the franchise is held together by its commitment to biblical authority, family values, and counter-cultural Christian witness. It retains a sense of being a gathered community at odds with the drift of mainstream Western Church and society. It remains small in England, but has strong links to Anglican and other Churches elsewhere, especially in parts of Africa.

5. JUSTICE AND PEACE
"Tackling poverty together"

It cares more about social than personal improvement. Most of its member churches are happy to be labelled "Christian anti-capitalist". Many of them focus on community organising, and there has been co-operation with the Roman Catholic Church since it returned to social teaching under Pope Francis.

6. OPEN CHURCH
"Go deeper"

Spiritual seekers and doubters have kept Open Church buoyant. It sits light to the "baggage" of religion, but tries to engage with the whole breadth of the Christian tradition — and other religions. Its emphasis on authenticity, and its refusal to prescribe lifestyles has proved popular with young people.

ALL OF these branches have established global links with other forms of Anglicanism, Christianity, and even other religions with which they have some alliance. They are responsible for their own finances and functioning.

Anyone can propose a new branch, and, over time, some will naturally wither while others will emerge. Individuals can belong to more than one. They may have to pay more to do so, but some have special introductory offers.

One great benefit of establishing a Church along these lines is that the energy currently invested in arguing about things such as gay marriage can be turned to constructive ends.

As the statistics I have presented in earlier sections show, the Church is at the end of a line — it has one last chance to win back disaffected "nominals" before they die out. By offering genuine variety, and labelling its congregations clearly, all existing affiliates — and their children and grandchildren — should at last be able to find a home, whether for occasional or more regular engagement.

Such a shift will force urgent structural reforms. Money and property are key. All the Church's properties — churches as well as clergy housing — need to be sold, or put into an independent not-for-profit trust. This releases effort and capital. Branches of the franchise can rent back what they need, on favourable terms. The whole C of E pension fund and liability can also be passed to an independent provider.

> 'The important thing to emphasise is that a cure is possible'

As for organisational structures, the already-dissolving parochial system will die a natural death. Each branch can devise its own governance structure, and make decisions for itself. This provides opportunities for lay Anglicans to work in genuine partnership with clergy.

EPISCOPACY will remain the guarantor of unity. A substantially reduced number of dioceses will each have a college of bishops, whose members are drawn from across the groups.

Two archbishoprics remain. Relieved of their impossible burdens, their occupants are free to play a symbolic part as a focus for religion and society — particularly in ritual roles, as modelled by the current monarch.

They stand for the whole Church — perhaps for all faiths in England — irrespective of their personal opinions. Statements and reports made on behalf of the entire C of E are not encouraged. "Prophetic" interventions are still possible, but not required.

The monarch continues to be the Supreme Governor of this essentially lay-led Church. It establishes greater accountability in its members, and the nation, by laying down its failed experiment in synodical government, and returning oversight of some areas to Parliament.

In these ways, the Church plays a more dynamic, but more modest, part in a country in which it is one among many other forms of Christian and non-Christian faith.

In terms of unity and discipline, there are a few features of the Anglican brand which all its branches must accept, but they are binding. These are thrashed out between them at the start of the process of restructuring. They represent the minimum requirements to be part of the established Church of England.

A FANTASY? Yes. But a fantasy that hints at the scale of the imagination and change that are needed to save a dying Church.

The important thing to emphasise is that a cure is still possible. The hopeful sign is that, despite its terrible injuries and neglect, the Church of England is still alive. It still offers a broad, varied, and interesting Christian approach to life, and a spirit of inclusive enquiry.

It allows God to speak through the whole breadth of Christian scripture and tradition, not just a small part of it. And it guards a unique blend of Christian, and English, cultures, which — for all its obvious flaws and failings — is still precious to those whose lives it inspires.

Can we grow? Yes we can

The Church is not in an inevitable spiral of decline: there is a realistic hope of growth, say David Goodhew and Bob Jackson

AT A conference on church-growth strategy last year, the Archbishop of Canterbury said that he saw no reason why the Church of England could not double in size in the next 15 to 25 years, provided it renewed its spirituality, forged stronger unity, and prioritised evangelism.

We agree that substantial church growth is possible. Studying the decline and growth of the Church of England leads us to conclude that there are solid grounds to hope that it will grow in the next two decades. Those who say that the Church will inevitably shrink rely on misleading generalisations, and questionable analysis. We base our confidence on four foundations:

I. THEOLOGY

GOD wants his Church to grow numerically. Only God grows the Church. Our job is to collaborate with him, and not get in his way. "Growth" in the Christian life means growth in holiness, and growth in service to society; but it also means the numerical growth of the Church.

The New Testament is full of positive references to numerical church growth. The core doctrines of Christian faith presuppose communities of believers growing numerically as the means by which faith is incarnated.

One of the Holy Spirit's key tasks is to be fuel for numerical church growth. It is surely no accident that those churches that most emphasise the Holy Spirit are the ones that are currently seeing the greatest numerical church growth.

Church history is littered with saints who grew the Church numerically: Cuthbert (who preached as well as prayed), Francis and the friars, Hannah More, and the Sunday school movement.

Taking numerical growth seriously enables churches to become fully sacramental. Often, the word "sacramental" is a synonym for "eucharistic". But that is to be only semi-sacramental. Many churches (High and Low) do not fully prioritise baptism.

Seeking numerical church growth has, as its natural corollary, a far greater emphasis on (and far more frequent administration of) baptism and confirmation. Such an emphasis makes us more sacramental — and more faithful to the practice of the historic Church.

Seeking the numerical growth of the Church is not something theologically disreputable, or mere pragmatism. When Christendom still existed, growing the Church could lead to oppressive behaviour. Now, when British élite culture is overwhelmingly secular, such a danger is much reduced.

Christians can unhelpfully play off "Kingdom" and "Church" as if they were separate, even antagonistic, realities. But that is bad exegesis. "Kingdom" is bigger than "Church", but they overlap. The Church is the sociological outworking of following Jesus. God the Holy Trinity wants his Church to grow numerically. We should not be embarrassed to seek the same goal. Numerical church growth is central to a balanced theology.

2. HARD DATA

EMPIRICAL research shows that there is significant church growth happening across England — as well as elsewhere inside the Church of England.

- Churches in Greater London, of all denominations, grew by 16 per cent between 2005 and 2012.
- The electoral roll of London diocese grew by more than 70 per cent in the two decades to 2010.
- There are now 2250 Messy Churches registered, and 350,000 to 550,000 people attending Messy Church across the denominations — there were none in 2004. Sixty per cent are Anglican.
- Across ten Anglican dioceses, there are 477 fresh expressions, whose combined attendance is 21,000.
- Weekly attendance at cathedrals rose by 35 per cent between 2002 and 2012.
- In a survey of 1700 churches, conducted by Professor David Voas for the Church Commissioners' church growth-research programme,

the majority of respondents stated that they had grown numerically in the years 2008 to 2013.

• The diocese of Leicester's average attendance by adults grew by 11 per cent from 2009 to 2012, and by children by 38 per cent.

No, it is not like this everywhere; but the existence of decline does not mean that we should ignore the growth that is taking place. At the very least, the situation looks patchy. But, overall, the numbers look to be on the turn.

Christians have been told so often that the Church is declining, and doomed to oblivion, that we easily internalise this message. The result is a kind of "decline theology", where Christianity is redefined so that numerical decline is assumed to be inevitable, even unproblematic.

Being concerned to grow numerically then becomes seen as somehow "bad form". Not only is this bad theology, there is much empirical data to rebut such fatalism.

Ten growth principles for every parish

1. Pray specifically for God to grow the Church numerically.
2. Intentionally, and persistently, seek numerical growth.
3. Create worship styles and facilities that are more diverse.
4. Create cultures that are inviting and welcoming.
5. Plant new congregations and fresh expressions.
6. Train leaders and congregations for growth.
7. Focus on the under-25s.
8. Shorten vacancies, and do vacancies better.
9. In multiply ministries: a 'focal minister' for every church.
10. Focus financial resources on areas of opportunity.

---

3. RESEARCH

RESEARCH over the past 15 years has given us a much better understanding of the key factors that lead to the growth of the churches. We know that churches and clergy who intentionally seek numerical growth see more growth than churches and clergy who do not.

We know that growing faith among under-25s is crucial to growth.

We know that churches that start new services, and plant new congregations, are more likely to grow.

We know that churches across the spectrum of traditions can grow. We know that, if you can raise up larger numbers of leaders (ordained or lay, paid or unpaid), churches are more likely to grow. And if you cut the number of clergy, churches are more likely to decline.

'God wants his Church to grow'

4. STRATEGY

THE Church of England is finding a new unity behind the priority to grow the Church numerically. Many churches have Mission Action Plans, and many dioceses have growth strategies.

Wherever we go around the country, we find that churches that have implemented good practices over a sustained period have grown numerically as a result. Whole dioceses that have had some sort of strategy in place for a while are beginning to grow consistently, year after year.

Top priority: discipling under-25s

All the research shows that most people who come to faith do so in the first 25 years of life. Of course, we should never give up on people after that point! But discipling under-25s is crucial for numerical growth. Here are six key steps:

1. Recognise that discipling under-25s is the top priority for every parish.
2. Start with Christian parents, who should see discipling children as central to parenting.
3. Focus resources: evidence shows a direct relationship between resourcing work with children, young people, and young adults, and numerical church growth.
4. Concentrate on teens and young adults – this is when people tend to fall away from faith.
5. Promote worship that involves children and young people.
6. Have a clear pathway of discipleship from Messy Church age to those aged 25.

FOLLOWING Christ is good news: it is purpose in a confusing world, forgiveness in a blame-filled world, and it is hope beyond death in a world afraid of its mortality. And God has so made us that following Jesus can be done only in community. It cannot be done on your own.

The most important reason why there is hope for numerical church growth is that God wants his Church to grow. In a culture where many voices that say church growth is impossible, or unnecessary, churches and leaders need a robust theology for numerical church growth.

God insists that we collaborate in his growing of the Church. And such partnership requires serious prayer, and the generation of a meaningful strategy — local, diocesan, and national. The top priority in that strategy is the discipling of under-25s.

To help us in such work, we should remember that the Church is not without wisdom on what makes for numerical growth. Every congregation, everyone of us who exercises ministry in the Church, can do something right now. There really is hope for the Church of England. A sizeable minority of the Anglican Church is already growing, and that could become the majority — if we work and pray to this end.

It's not just about the numbers

The Church of England has an unhealthy fixation on numerical growth, says *Martyn Percy*. We should be more concerned with quality, not quantity

THE beguiling attraction of the very first Christian heresies and heterodoxies lay in their simplicity. They presented the most attractive solution to any immediate and apparently unsolvable problems. For the first generations of Christians, these usually lay in the sphere of doctrine and praxis.

For us as a Church today, the presenting problem appears to be declining numbers in our congregations. *Ergo*, an urgent emphasis on numerical church growth must be the answer.

Right, surely? But wrong, actually. The first priority of the Church is to follow Jesus Christ. This may be a costly calling, involving self-denial, depletion, and death. Following Jesus may not lead us to any numerical growth.

We are to love the Lord with all our heart, mind, soul, and strength, and our neighbours as ourselves. There is no greater commandment. So the numerical growth of the Church cannot be a greater priority than the foundational mandate set before us by Jesus.

Karl Barth observed, more than 50 years ago, that the true growth of the Church is not to be thought of in mainly extensive terms, but rather those that are intensive. He argued that the vertical (or intensive) growth of the Church does not necessarily lead to extensive numerical growth. He went on to say that "we cannot, therefore, strive for vertical renewal merely to produce a wider audience."

Barth concluded that, if the Church and its mission were used only as a means of extensive growth, the inner life of the Church lost its meaning and power: "The Church can be fulfilled only for its own sake, and then — unplanned and unarranged — it will bear its own fruits."

Many parish clergy, and those working in all kinds of sector ministries, already know this to be true. The Church does not exist to

127

grow exponentially. Mission is deeper than that. The Church exists to be the body of Christ.

THE pastoral theologian Eugene Peterson once said that the one thing he had learned in mission and ministry was how complex measurable growth could be. He draws on the theologian, essayist, poet, and farmer, Wendell Berry, learning that "parish work is every bit as physical as farm work — it is about these people, at this time, under these conditions."

The pastoral turn towards an agrarian motif is arresting. Jesus told a number of parables about growth, and they are all striking for their simplicity and surprise, especially the allegory of the sower. This should probably be the template for all diocesan Mission Action Plans,

THE PARABLE OF THE SOWER
DEMONSTRATED AT THE 10 A.M.

PATH

SOME HEAR THE MESSAGE
BUT DO NOT UNDERSTAND IT

ROCKY GROUND

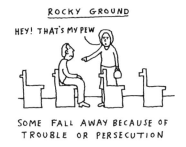

SOME FALL AWAY BECAUSE OF
TROUBLE OR PERSECUTION

THORNS

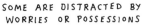

SOME ARE DISTRACTED BY
WORRIES OR POSSESSIONS

GOOD SOIL

SOME BRING FRIENDS:
ONE HUNDRED, OR SIXTY, OR THIRTY

because Jesus is saying to the Church, "Have regard for your neighbour's context and conditions.

So, you might work in a parish with the richest soil, where every seed planted springs to life, where the seasons are kind, the vegetation lush, the harvest plentiful. But some places are stony ground, and faithful mission and ministry in that field might be picking out the rocks for several generations.

'God's maths is different from ours'

The question the parable throws back to the Church is this: what kind of growth can you expect from the ground and conditions you work with? This is where our current unilateral emphasis on numerical church growth can be so demoralising and disabling.

Is it really the case that every leader of numerical church growth is a more spiritually faithful and technically gifted pastor than his or her less successful neighbour? The parable says "no" to this.

I mention this for one very obvious reason: if we continue to place the heterodoxy of numerical growth at the heart of the Church, we risk eroding our character, and our morale.

SOME WILL argue that if you aim at nothing, you will hit it every time. Better to have a target and a plan than just keep plodding on.

Maybe. The Charge of the Light Brigade had vision, courage, objectives, and some strategy; but the rest, as they say, is history.

So, the key to understanding numerical church growth might be to engage in deeper and more discerning readings of our contexts — the soil we seek to nourish and bless — so the seeds can flourish. There is work to be done on the ground.

Factors producing numerical church growth and decline are always complex. But the Church might need to do some basic maths. In the secular world, one plus one equals two. But counting whole numbers in the Church is not straightforward.

Is a newly baptised infant one unit, in terms of believers? Does the person who comes every week, but has more doubt than faith, count as one, or a half? Is the regular, but not frequent churchgoer, one, or less than one? And what about the person who comes to everything at church, but has a heart of stone?

We know that God counts generously. The poor, the lame, the sick, the sinners — all seem to be promised a whole seat at God's table in his Kingdom. That is why Jesus was seldom interested in quantity; the Kingdom is about small numbers, and enriching quality.

Fortunately, God is loving enough to tell us plenty of counter-cultural stories about numbers: leaving the 99 and going after one, for example.

God's maths is different from ours. No one denies the urgency of mission, or the need for the Church to address numerical growth. But the Church exists to glorify God, and follow Jesus Christ. After that it may grow, or it may not. Faithfulness must always be put before the search for success.

OF COURSE, we need leaders who can ride the cultural waves of our time. But we also need other leaders who can read the tides, and the deeper cultural currents of our age. Our recent emphasis on numerical church growth has led to the unbalanced ascendancy of mission-minded middle-managers.

It is hard to imagine a Michael Ramsey, William Temple, or Edward King receiving preferment in the current climate. The veneration of growth squeezes out the space for broader gifts in leadership that can nourish the Church and engage the world.

As with all things Anglican, it is a question of balance. There are no bad foods, only bad diets. And the continued over-emphasis of numerical growth skews the weight and measure in the body of our leadership.

This is a more subtle disproportion than it might at first appear. It was said of the late Cardinal Basil Hume that "he had the gift of being able to talk to the English about God without making them wish they were somewhere else." The value of this gift should not be underestimated.

And, for our national mission, this is precisely why we need a leadership that incorporates space for the holy and devout: the gentle pastor, the poet and the prophet, the teacher and the theologian — and possibly a radical or two for good measure.

The Church may not always draw near to such leaders. But the nation often does — especially those who do not usually go to church. For the first time since the Reformation, we now have no bishops who have held a university post in theology. The nation may not notice this explicitly, but, at a subliminal level, it will certainly sense the lack.

So, for the sake of national mission, and our credibility, we may want to intentionally develop a broader range of leaders than the singular objective of numerical church growth currently allows for.

BUT let us return to numbers. There are some anomalies. The 2010/11 Church Statistics show that many dioceses that had well-developed mission strategies showed continuing numerical decline.

Perhaps the greatest surprise was to discover one diocese that had enjoyed significant numerical growth — a whopping 17 per cent in average weekly and usual Sunday attendance. Ironically, this was led by a bishop who had seemingly little in the way of experience in mission and ministry.

Like Basil Hume, the bishop had not been a parish priest, and could not tick any of the boxes that indicated he had led any congregation to numerical growth.

The diocese was Canterbury. And the bishop was someone who also had the gift of being able to talk about God in public. Having a knack for imaginative, reflective, and refractive public theology and spirituality does, indeed, intrigue and draw people in who might not otherwise pay attention to the rumour of God.

By welcoming some teachers, poets, and prophets among our leadership, who point us imaginatively and compellingly, to Christ, we might yet discover an even richer, more effective purpose in our mission. And, in so doing, we might find some other routes to numerical growth along the way.

We need to reconstruct the Church

John Tuckett says that time is running out for the
Church of England. It requires organisational transformation
if it is to survive

ALL organisations like to claim that they are "unique". The Church of
England is no exception. But how unique is the Church compared with
other public organisations that work for the public good?

My experience is with large-scale-change programmes in the public
sector, such as the NHS and the Ministry of Defence, and the part I am
playing currently is to bring about the dissolution of three dioceses in
West Yorkshire, and create a new entity.

I am no theologian, but my experience across many public and not-for-
profit organisations does qualify me to consider how the Church, with its
Christian outlets in every community, its many staff (paid and unpaid),
and budgets of many millions of pounds, contrasts with similar bodies.

My approach is to assess the "fitness" of the Church to thrive in the 21st
century, by holding up three "mirrors" that represent the hallmarks of a
modern agile organisation.

Mirror One: A compelling vision with clear goals which are achievable

UNDOUBTEDLY, there are plenty of national aspirations — the current goals of spiritual and numerical growth being promoted by the
Archbishops and General Synod are among them — but arguably there
is no overarching vision or Church-wide strategy to deliver outcomes
that are increasingly the norm of other organisations.

Does this matter? If the Church is happy for its total output to be the
sum of what each diocese achieves on its own, then, perhaps, no.

Looking at what the Church is achieving now, the trends on in-
dicators such as congregation sizes and levels of giving are static or
downwards. Public demand for what the Church currently offers is a
very different picture from the ever-growing demand for, say, NHS and

local-authority services. This may seem an unfair comparison, but how an organisation's outputs are sought, whatever their nature, says much about their relevance.

Mirror Two: A simple structure with clear lines of accountability, and responsibility at all levels

THE structure of the Church, with its 44 dioceses linked to a "centre" of General Synod, Archbishops' Council, et al., seems straightforward. But add other central Church House departments, Lambeth and Bishopthorpe Palaces, and the autonomous nature of a diocese, and understanding just who is responsible for what becomes more complex.

Within a diocese, the mass of committees, boards, and sub-committees, coupled with the synodical structure at diocesan and deanery levels, makes it especially challenging to identify where responsibility and accountability actually lie.

In such situations, decision-making will "float" from one level to another, making for bureaucratic, slow processes that are a far cry from any modern norm of best practice. There is also a risk that the valuable resources donated by the public are supporting inefficient organisations, and are not being used to best effect.

Mirror Three: The culture and values that drive decision-making

DECISION-MAKING processes within the Church show three prominent characteristics. The first is representation. Every part of the Church has a say in key decisions, through elected representatives, whether at synods or in the many diocesan boards and committees, often enshrined in Church Measures, but this makes for numerically very large, and potentially unwieldy bodies.

The second is a strong desire for consensus — doing everything possible to ensure that everyone agrees.

The third is historical heritage and maintaining continuity — only stopping something as a final resort. (Here, the Church is similar to the NHS, which still agonises over stopping ongoing health-care in order to reinvest elsewhere.)

THESE characteristics can result in high levels of commitment when decisions are finally made. But decision-making can be time-consuming, and inherently opposed to radical change. In comparison with other organisations, two characteristics are noticeably less apparent.

First, ensuring that relevant skills and expertise are available to address complex issues, and that competency is as important as representation. Second, the use of evidence from research or performance-management processes to inform decision-making. There are signs of this emerging, but the Church has a long way to go in catching up with contemporary counterparts.

The evidence of the three mirrors, taken together, suggests that the Church has significant issues to address that are of a system-wide nature, and affect all parts of the Church.

Is restructuring — changing boundaries and the numbers of bodies, so often favoured by organisations — the solution? My experience is that restructuring only has real benefits when it enables people to do things in new ways, to achieve new results.

Restructuring for the sake of it is like rearranging deck chairs on the *Titanic*, and many restructurings in the public sector failed because they were responses to short-term financial, or political, pressures, without new goals or ways of working.

If restructuring is not the answer, then we enter the realms of significant organisational transformation, whereby the entire "system" of the Church is overhauled and renewed.

'It needs to plan radical change sooner rather than later'

This is what is happening in West Yorkshire, where the complete dissolution of three dioceses is, in effect, a letting-go of the past and outdated practices as far as is possible, in order to allow a rebuilding and reinvention of how a diocese works.

A TRANSFORMATION agenda for the Church as a whole would focus on three aspects:

1. Constructing a meaningful vision for the Church, using tangible measurable outcomes, and success factors that demonstrate progress and what change is being achieved.

2. Deciding the critical processes that the Church wishes to use in achieving its vision; and in this, being radical, and going beyond "simplifying" into reinvention.

3. Designing a system that supports and enables, with clear accountabilities and responsibilities, with all parts working together so the output is greater than the sum of its parts.

Transformation on this scale for a complete system is rarely undertaken, and must be carefully planned, and the implications thought through. This requires expertise the Church does not have, yet would have to be acquired and paid for.

This is not work for well-meaning amateurs. Also, any change must be driven from the top, with the commitment of all at the top. Anything less only results in subterfuge and dissension — undermining implementation.

Furthermore, radical change affects everyone. No one can stand aside and say, "This is not for me". Finally, transformation needs confidence to move forward without knowing all the answers in advance

— with a willingness to enjoy confusion as being the source of new thinking.

SOME organisations wait for an external event, like a change of government or financial crisis, to precipitate major change. This is high risk, as the event is often more draconian than was ever imagined or wanted. In this case, organisations are left running to catch up, no longer in charge of their own destiny.

Successful organisations initiate radical change themselves, while they are still on the "up". They recognise that there is aways a need for revitalisation, and re-invention, and that to carry on as before while expecting a different outcome is organisational insanity.

The Church may not be on the "up" but — if it is not to be dictated to by events, or governments — it needs to start planning major radical change sooner, not later. Time is running out. The real question is not whether such change should be adopted, but can the Church afford not to?

How unique does the Church want to be? It can claim that it is so different from other organisations that their experience can be ignored, and it can carry on as before.

Or else the Church can show the world how unique it really is, by having the courage, the confidence, and the faith to take organisational transformation way beyond what many others do — and explore new ways in which it professes the Christian faith.

It's time to change, and fast

The Church of England needs to relate to the whole of the nation, *Charles Clarke* argues — but this has five primary implications

BY THE year 2035, the Church of England needs fully to embrace the diversity of modern life and society in the United Kingdom.

I would say that this is desirable for any faith that is more than a sect or faction. For the Established Church of this country, however, it is more than desirable — it is essential. The Church of England will risk losing the status and privileges of establishment unless it can demonstrate that it deserves them by relating to all of British society, in all of its diversity.

This has five substantive implications. In each, the Church has already been changing for some years, but the change needs to go faster, and become more comprehensive.

First, the Church of England needs, in its own conduct and behaviour, to reflect its positive recognition of the value and importance of diversity. The barren and depressing debates about the place of women in the Church, the rights of gay people, and other similar matters need firmly to have become history.

Since I am not a theist, I am unqualified to offer theological comment; but, second, it seems to me that the Church of England needs to move beyond particular doctrinal standpoints which ultimately result from its Tudor foundation.

Over nearly 500 years, doctrinal conflicts have both defined difference with other Churches and spawned conflict within the Church. Whatever their historical justification, the Church now needs to focus on what unites, far more than what divides.

THIRD, this means that the Church has to become not only the defender of its own faith, but a far broader-based defender of respect for faith — all faiths — throughout our national life. This means working even harder to develop functioning and working relationships both with other faiths and with all those individuals and groups who have their own faiths, without adhering rigidly to any collective church doctrine.

And, fourth, the Church needs to understand how best to express these values in its broad relationship to the rest of society, in areas such as the constitutional position of the Church, its influence in education and welfare, and its promotion of strong and cohesive local communities.

'The Church must focus on what unites it'

The Church of England's fifth challenge is how to exist in an even more diverse and complicated world, in which many of its component national Churches have quite different parts to play in their own societies, and so, unsurprisingly, have different approaches to these problems. A difficult process of dialogue and devolution is the only way to make progress here, and avoid damaging schism.

The Church has already been moving — usually slowly — in each of these areas, but change needs to be accelerated dramatically if the centrality of the Church of England to our society is to be demonstrated, and establishment justified.

This is all a huge challenge, but if the Church does not succeed, it will make itself less and less relevant to society, and this will, in turn, place in question the very idea of an Established Church.

Word and action hand in hand

Evangelism needs to address people's felt needs — physical as well as spiritual, says *Elizabeth Oldfield*

THE primary challenge for the Church of England for the next 20 years is a simple, if not an easy one. It is the need to create churches where people who have no heritage of Christianity can encounter God.

We all know that faith is no longer being passed down, and must instead be offered afresh. The obvious answer to this is evangelism — a focus on growth has certainly been increasingly obvious in wider church strategy. However, this has often distracted attention, ironically, from what should be evangelism's essential and indivisible partner: social action.

It is increasingly obvious that, as Angus Ritchie of the Contextual Theology Centre says, we are moving into an era of "both/and" Christianity, when neither personal conversion nor serving the needs of our communities holds primary sway. The dichotomy has always been a false one, and I hope that in 20 years time we will see a Church where it is eroded entirely.

The reality of how shortsighted it is to separate these two has been hammered home for me during research for a project that the think tank Theos is undertaking for the Church Urban Fund, looking at churches in areas of high deprivation who are genuinely serving the common good.

Although the research is not focused on growth, we have found that — rather than social projects like food banks, debt advice centres, elderly engagement, or youth work detracting from the church's effort to bring people into their congregations — it aids them.

These projects provide a first point of contact with many for whom Alpha courses or "guest services" are initially completely alien ideas. In the case of one church in the north-west, I spoke to residents who had got to know this incredibly loving, outward-looking community through their gardening club, or child-contact centre, and have slowly been drawn into becoming a member of the congregation.

ALPHA courses and their equivalents are often important at this stage, creating a bridge for those who come to belong, even loosely, to a community, to move towards believing.

This cannot, and should not, be the aim of serving the needs of the community. This approach only creates instrumentalised relationships. When social action and the desire to introduce people to God work well together, however, they flow from the same heart — an organic, Kingdom-building, deeply transformative process.

That church in the north-west has grown, unspectacularly, often painfully, but steadily, as, one by one, people see something different there — and, as it grows, it has served the surrounding area in astonishing ways. It has created nourishing and generous spaces that are not quite "church" and not quite "world" — fruitful in themselves and, for some, the entry point to a personal faith.

'It may need serious structural thinking' If, in 20 years' time, every church was this active and visible in its local community, slowly and patiently drawing people in through its hospitality, and compelling community, I'd be thrilled.

Many already are, but others are too focused on the narrative of decline, burdened with financially draining buildings, wearied by internal bureaucracy, and sheer lack of "boots on the ground", as Professor Linda Woodhead has said.

Making this happen may require some serious structural rethinking. A less precious attitude to buildings, where appropriate, might help, as would training in theological colleges in fund-raising, charity law, empowering volunteers, and all the other skills these kind of churches now require. The Church, overall, would be more locally focused, and humbler, but also more hopeful.

It's all about the parish

We need to hold on to parish-centred ministry that has education at its heart, says *Alison Milbank*

IT IS ironic that, at the very time that market-forces, bureaucracy, and even the weather make the need for intermediate institutions ever more necessary, the parish is under threat as a costly, outmoded model rather than an inestimable and flexible resource.

In the recent flooding in Muchelney, Somerset, the parish church has provided support and liturgy; and in the city it continues to be a refuge for the homeless and the immigrant. We all need community, and especially one rooted not in utility, but in relation to the final ends of human life. What else can include us all, simply as people?

The parish I dream of in the future will be utterly outward-looking, opening its doors to the needs of all local people of every creed and background — library, kitchen, credit union, cinema, advice centre, and social meeting-place — but also richer in terms of prayer, theological study, and Christian formation.

Parishes succeed where the clergy and the people believe in what they are doing, and trust the gospel of Christ as truly compelling. A vaguely apologetic approach to the faith has yielded us nothing but drift, and has allowed the secular world to infect us with its own nihilism. Those who fantasise that the parish is out of date evade the fact that this is because Christianity itself is being rejected.

We are in a war, and the battle must be fought with all the resources of intellect and imagination that we can muster. Art, poetry, drama, dance, and music of the highest quality must be used to make our liturgical life deeper and more sustaining.

ABOVE all, we need education at every level — from toddlers to theological colleges — that is grounded in scripture, Christian philosophy, and the riches of our Hebraic and classical tradition.

This will make us more effective evangelists and critics of social injustice, and, paradoxically, more able to deal with future challenges. I have seen a mixed group of people utterly gripped by the applicability of the Didache, and Athanasius, to their own lives. Theology in the pub has also been shown to work.

'We need churches that act as a sacral space'

Many in our own congregations are denied the food that would sustain their faith at work, and at home. The truth is that they have lost credal belief, and no longer understand that to be a Christian means being inducted through the eucharistic representation of the incarnation into a participation in the life of the Trinity. Only when church members have been empowered with the gospel can outreach have meaning.

I long for openness and hospitality combined with a recovery of theological poise. A consistent but variegated programme of Christian habit and beliefs should infuse every Anglican school, college, and institution.

We need churches that act as the sacral focus for a specific place, and represent it in both strong intercession and practical action. Money and people will never come — and, indeed, will drain away — unless we have confidence in the Church as our salvation.

Turn Jesus right side up

The Church must tell of a Saviour who is at home in our cities as well as the suburbs, says *James Jones*

ALTHOUGH we celebrate the birth of the Church at Pentecost, I have always thought that the nativity was a serious rival. This was the first gathering to worship Christ. Anyone looking to the future of the Church should keep this scene clearly in their rear-view mirror.

The characters of the nativity give clues to the character of an authentic Christian community. Here, a woman feeds the body of Christ, which is a priestly and episcopal vocation. If a woman can feed the body of Jesus in the flesh, she can surely feed the body of Christ in the Spirit. A Church where women, with men, minister with unqualified authority and opportunity will best express the human face of God, in whose image both women and men are equally created.

To the nativity came seekers from the East: they were not the most obvious candidates to worship Christ first, and their presence was a sign of a God without frontiers. The Christian community was never to be defined by nationality.

The point was reinforced by the adult Christ, whose cleansing of the Temple was not so much a rant against commercialism as a rage against racism: "My house shall be for all races." The Church of England, a Church of and for the nation, has yet to express the diversity of the country and become "a house of prayer for all races".

The coming of the shepherds proves to me the historicity of the story. Nobody would choose such disreputable rogues to endorse their message. Their presence signalled God's bias to the poor, with whom Mary's child would share his life.

But have you ever wondered why, in the time of Jesus, the working classes flocked to him, and the middle classes shunned him? And why, in our day, the middle classes fill our suburban churches, and the working classes give him a wide berth? An exaggeration, I know, but with enough to it to make us ask what we have done to Jesus to turn him on his head. An authentic Church of the future must look for genuine growth in the leafless landscapes.

THAT first gathering around Jesus saw him lying in a manger. The angels gave clues to find him: "A child wrapped in bands of cloth" — hardly a distinguishing feature for a baby. But "lying in a manger" is unusual and resonant. For he, in his own words, would one day say that he was bread, fodder for life.

There was a risk in putting a child in a feeding trough, presumably with animals around. Yet his lying there beckoned a coming world of new relationships between all God's creatures, where, to the surprise of shepherds, even the wolf and the lamb would lie down together.

'The working classes flocked to Jesus'

An authentic Church will express a new attitude to creation in which "all things have come into being through and for Christ."

These are some of the fresh expressions of an authentic Church of the future.

A matter of confidence

The Church of England needs to emphasise
youth, unity, evangelism, faithfulness — and speed,
says *Graham Tomlin*

OVER the next 20 years, we should aim to have a healthy, attractive, outward-looking Anglican Christian community within reach of every person or household in England.

We might imagine a national Church confident enough in the gospel to offer a more communal, and less individualistic, vision of life than that of the society around it, using its voice in favour of the disadvantaged, and building a reputation for locally based action.

It would have representatives capable of making the case for Christian faith publicly. I hope, by then, we will also have found healthy ways to live together with our disagreements over women bishops, gay marriage, and whatever issues come up in 2034.

What needs to happen to bring this about? For a start, the parish system will need further adaptation, as has happened throughout its history, to make innovation less difficult. Church partnerships, where larger churches partner with struggling ones to renew old buildings, and reinvigorate congregations — as has happened, for example, with Holy Trinity, Brompton, and its network — will be part of the story.

Churches of any tradition that experience growth need to be encouraged, and enabled to reproduce that life in other contexts, with government grants to help maintain and renew the national heritage of ancient church buildings.

At the same time, smaller, ground-up, indigenous-led plants also need to be encouraged. We hear too many stories of new church-plants or Fresh Expressions that have to endure endless energy- and vision-sapping committees, and legal processes. Due scrutiny and consultation are good, but when they slow down progress to a snail's pace, the process needs to be simplified.

CONFIDENT, creative evangelism needs to become much more part of the church's natural modus vivendi. Alpha has been one of the most remarkable gifts from the Church of England to the worldwide Church over the past few decades.

We need the same urgency and vision that created Alpha to keep adapting it for a fast-changing world, create imaginative new pathways for people to find faith in the future, and be more deliberate about training younger Anglicans as public apologists.

Speaking of youth — the average age of a British Muslim is 25, while that of Anglicans is about 61. Research tells us that, to attract young people, you need younger priests. We need to attract younger ordinands, and build systems of training that enable them effectively to complete curacies alongside initial training, so they are able to move into leadership and incumbency positions earlier.

And, in all this, unity is vital. We need strong Catholic and Evangelical churches, each with their own strengths, working missionally and as friends. And that means training our ordinands together more than we do at present. The depressing sniping between traditions is fatal to mission.

'To attract young people, you need young priests'

Who would ever trust a group of people (let alone their God) who cannot resist tearing each other apart?

And do not think for a moment that it will be easy. As Henri de Lubac put it: "If the Church were more faithful to her mission, she would doubtless be the more loved, more listened to, and more persecuted."

Simply spell out the Word

The C of E's health depends on explaining the plain and straightforward meaning of the Bible, says *Susie Leafe*

I AM convinced of one thing: it is the Word that does the work.

If we are to ensure that, in 20 years' time, the Church of England has a strong and credible witness in every community in our nation, we need to stop believing that growth depends on particular programmes or traditions, on brilliant leadership, or community projects, and instead depend on the Word made flesh, and the Word written to do the work.

More than 20 years ago, many of those who founded Reform were challenged to look again at the way they taught God's Word. They learned to preach in a way that laid bare the meaning of the text rather than impose meaning on it. They learned to preach the meta-narrative of the Bible, and not just individual verses or doctrines.

Perhaps they learned something of what Luke describes Jesus as doing on the Emmaus road: "And beginning with Moses and all the prophets, he explained to them what was said in all the scriptures concerning himself."

The results are interesting. Our analysis shows that the 350 or so churches represented by Reform have bucked many of the trends of the past 20 years. One third of their average congregation is under the age of 30. One third of churches have experienced sufficient growth to require them to start a new congregation in the past ten years.

Their average weekly attendance is three times that of the average C of E church. They produce three times the average number of ordinands.

I WAS surprised to find that the location of churches represented by

Reform reflects, almost exactly, the socio-economic profile of the nation. It is not resources or youth that has grown these churches: on the contrary, they have resources and young people because that is what they have grown to be.

The job is not complete. Our churches are gatherings of sinful human beings. We get things wrong. But — dependent on the forgiveness offered by Jesus's death and resurrection — we seek to live lives transformed and shaped by his Word.

Teaching and preaching is not the "end game", but it is the means by which we are pointed back to the Word that equips us for every good work. Consequently, we pray for bishops who uphold sound and wholesome doctrine, and we continue to train all those who teach — male or female, lay or ordained — to "properly handle the word of truth".

'We pray for bishops who uphold sound doctrine'

The *Church Times* has laid out a bleak picture of the future of the Church of England. It is true that we face many challenges. But, surely, Reform's experience is great news.

Any church or diocese that wishes to see growth could make systematic, relevant, expository preaching its priority. Why don't we just let the Word do the work?

A Church *for* England

Anna Norman-Walker believes that, for the institution to thrive, it may need to die first

I AM due to retire in 20 years' time. It is very likely that my generation, and those who come after us, will have to ride the wave of the collapse of the Church of England in its present form.

Short of an unprecedented Anglican revival, the demand on us to adapt and change is unavoidable. So, I ponder the sort of Church of England that I would like to retire from serving. It would be one that had survived the painful transition from the centre to the edge — yet was fruitful and distinctive enough be a credible player in society, and known as a force for good. A "Church for England", at the very least.

Buildings — our great white elephant

WE WILL continue to offer sacred spaces through many of our ancient buildings, but these spaces will be used creatively and flexibly. Rural churches will be places to mark life's journey, and celebrate the seasonal festivals, with local market-town "minsters" continuing to offer the wider ministry of the Church's life, supporting and enabling locally disseminated mission.

Many urban churches also will have become servants of community life, but in different ways, hosting libraries, night shelters, day nurseries, cafés, and pubs.

Some will continue to serve the worshipping communities that gather there, but "churches" will be found in a whole variety of places, not least within networks of human community, unrestrained by geography.

Worship and witness — our purpose

THERE will be High, Low, and somewhere-in-the-middle churches — critically, their shared identity will be found in being outward-looking centres of mission whose life of worship, witness and service is diverse, intergenerational, multi-coloured, and refuses to ignore the poor. Cathedrals will have adopted a stronger identity as "mother churches", not only as centres of excellence in worship, but as a critical, educational, and evangelistic arm of the wider Church, and playing a vital part in civic life.

We will be widely known as communities of prayer, where all are welcome, and where Christ is shared in word and sacrament. We will be communities where people laugh loudly, live well, and shout out in one voice against injustice in all its forms. And our voice will be heard.

That, at its most basic level, is how I would like to see the Church of England expressing its life when I retire in 2036, but it is hard to imagine how we might get there when our structures and finances militate against it.

Radical and courageous leadership will surely help. The swallowing of a "reality pill" by the Victorian Society, English Heritage, and even the Government may strengthen the hope of our buildings' genuinely serving future society in any meaningful way, other than as museums.

Ultimately, I have little fear for the future life of the body of Christ in our nation in 20 years' time. People will continue to fall for Jesus, and witness to his love and mercy effectively in community, and many will be doing it in an Anglican way.

Some may even be beneficiaries of generous local "grants for mission" from the structure that rises from the ashes of the old Church of England.

Read the signs of the times

The Church needs to map its future on the basis of what we can see happening already, says *Maggi Dawn*

IT IS a common exercise in planning the future to envisage where you will be in ten or 20 years' time. Predicting the future is a precarious business, but imagining it has an honourable history.

The prophets of the Old Testament did it, but they did not map the future out of nothing. They read the signs of the times, and looked back at where they had come from, in order to imagine a better future. Like the prophets of old, we might read the present and the past in order to see the way ahead.

I live in the United States, from where it is easy to see the public impression of the Church, filtering out the experience of daily reality. If I believed the press, I would think that the Church of England is hopelessly riven by rows over women, LGBT concerns, and international disagreements. Yet the truth is that the Church has experienced great areas of growth, and vitality over the past 20 years.

In 1994, theological colleges were adopting a management model for priestly formation which reduced the understanding of priesthood as a sacramental role, and failed to promote lay ministry. Twenty years later, we would do well to abandon that model.

But there were signs of new life in 1994, too: the first women were ordained to the priesthood, and outside, or on the periphery of, the Church of England, "alternative worship" groups were springing up all over the country. Since then, the Church has embraced these, and introduced new models of ministry training to sustain them. In the mean time, cathedrals have experienced a new influx of visitors — tourists who become pilgrims — and here, too, are signs of hope.

LOOKING forward, rather than try get people to conform to tradition, I think we should observe where spiritual life is growing, and encourage it by finding ways to make the riches of the faith accessible to those who are searching for truth, community, and spiritual connection.

We need to allow priests to be sacramental ministers rather than managers; acknowledge and empower the huge, but under-utilised range of lay ministries in our communities; cut out unnecessary bureaucracy; and nurture signs of new life wherever they appear.

In this way we can continue the great tradition of Anglicanism, which, for four centuries, has held together varieties of expression and interpretation around a common core. The world needs the mystery of Anglo-Catholic worship, the inspiration of cathedral grandeur, the participatory experience of community in rural and urban congregations, the innovative mission of alternative, pioneer communities, and the social action of our mission organisations.

'We should observe where spirtual life is growing, and encourage it'

It is the tendency of dying institutions to close ranks, fiercely protecting an ever-narrowing tradition. If the Church of England can summon up the courage to be generous rather than legalistic, imaginative rather than bureaucratic, theologically astute rather than doctrinaire, then I believe that spiritual life will continue to flourish.

The press tells us the bad news, but we know the good news. We can afford to be generous and hopeful — in fact, we can't afford not to.

Back to basics and belief

Peter Ould envisages a future Church that, born out of crisis, returns to its true purpose

THE coronation of King William V was held on an auspicious day: 24 April 2034. A week of sun in the run-up to Easter had meant that the outdoor Good Friday service in Trafalgar Square was well attended, and the Archbishop of Canterbury, the Most Revd Katie Tupling, had preached a powerful sermon in the presence of the King, Queen, and Prince George.

Up and down the country, the churches were full on Easter Day, as congregations showed another record rise in attendances. Not since the 1970s had the pews been so full, and millions prayed for the reign of their new king.

Twenty years earlier, the picture had been remarkably different. In the midst of the second failed vote on women bishops, and the collapse of the "Croft discussions" on human sexuality, schism had looked the Church of England square in the face — until the fateful General Synod of July 2017.

When the late Archbishop Welby had begun his presidential address — "Communities of holiness, centres of resurrection" — no one had expected what came next. After the second great credit-crunch earlier that year (accompanied by the dramatic TV pictures of the rioting in European capitals), the former oil executive told the gathered clergy and laity that it was time to refocus.

"The internal battles of the past few decades have distracted us from the core mission of the Church," he said. "It is time, once again, to do what the Early Church did so well — simply preach Christ crucified and risen, and love the world around us that has lost sight of any vision, both politically and spiritually.

"There is no place for agendas, there is only space for the work of serving God, and serving the people we live among. Anything else is not what the Church of England is about."

FACED with a House of Bishops that closed ranks on the desire of some to advance their particular causes, some lobby groups found themselves frozen out, financially and socially.

The second generation Pilgrim Course (written by a retired archbishop, Dr Sentamu, and Bishop Michael Langrish) was a radical rewrite, focusing on a simple but effective basic discipleship. It was endorsed by Holy Trinity, Brompton, and by the GAFCON Primates, as the official follow-on from Alpha.

'It is time simply to preach Christ crucified and risen, and love the world'

But the one thing that really turned the Church around was the way that the United Ecclesiastical Credit Union stepped into the breach after the failure of the Royal Bank of Scotland, in 2023. With nowhere else to turn, millions of men and women moved their money into the hands of church-sponsored local banks, and put their dinner plates in the hands of locally resourced foodbanks (the four million unemployed were extremely grateful).

Suddenly, in the midst of a national malaise, the ordinary men and women of England saw a Church of England that knew what it believed (even if it was often at odds with the Government), and lived out a genuine public life of love.

In his address to the nation on Easter Monday, King William paid tribute to "the Church of our people that has walked alongside each of us over the past decade, through our pain and joy, just like the Saviour whom the Church and I serve."

And, as Archbishop Tupling settled with a cognac in her chair, watching it on her holographic TV, she joined the people of England in giving thanks for all God's mercies over the past 20 years.

Different visions of the Church's future

by Paul Handley

"SOMEONE had blundered." In one of the articles about where the Church of England might go next, the author recalls the Charge of the Light Brigade as a warning against pursuing the wrong vision. By deliberately choosing a wide range of authors for this health check, we present readers with a similarly large range of visions. Professor Woodhead suggests that different traditions within the Church distance themselves from each other and pursue the vision that suits them best. Other authors produce a composite vision that might do for all traditions, or promote a particular vision that, they argue, is the one that will turn the Church around.

Readers will naturally warm to the remedies that accord with their own spirituality and ecclesiology, but the point is that all the suggestions here have merit. Attention to the Bible, diligence in the sacraments, a deepening holiness, more effective social action, a willingness to unite with those outside the Anglican fold, a radical slimming down of bureaucracy, creativity in worship, the pursuit of theological understanding, intelligent shared leadership, joyful friendliness — each of these on its own would be the mark of a church's health. It is together, though, that they form the characteristics of a thriving national Church, which is what the Church of England still strives to be.

We are drawn back to St Paul's image of the Church as the body of Christ, made up of different members with different gifts, but inseparable to the extent that all will suffer harm if any is severed. And there is not one of these gifts that is not being practised within the Church of England today. These are the grounds for optimism expressed by most of our contributors — and for frustration that the Church is still so far away from where it might be. This is not just an impression, a question of poor PR, remedied by ignoring criticism and accentuating the positive. There have been too many blunders; there

155

are too many dysfunctional bits of the institution, and we hear from too many unhappy workers within it, not least among the bishops and clergy. Gifts are not nurtured, poor performance is unchecked, pastoral opportunities are neglected, and — continually — the Church's reputation is damaged. The purpose of this book was to expose those things that hinder growth — spiritual growth as well as numerical — and to help the Church to focus on ways to free the gifts that are too often being frustrated. Vision is important, for without it the various programmes and mission action plans detailed here are simply extra burdens. But what would the Church not be able to do if it held before it at all times the vision of Christ's love for his people?